The

ELOQUENT
ESSAY

OTHER PERSEA ANTHOLOGIES

The

ELOQUENT
ESSAY

AN ANTHOLOGY
OF CLASSIC & CREATIVE
NONFICTION

Edited, with an introduction by

JOHN LOUGHERY

A KAREN AND MICHAEL BRAZILLER BOOK

PERSEA BOOKS/NEW YORK

To Helen Loughery,

and to my students and colleagues—inestimable people—

at the Nightingale-Bamford School

Since this page cannot legibly accommodate all copyright notices,
pages 191–192 constitute an extension of the copyright page.

Copyright © 2000 by John Loughery

Requests for permission to reprint or to make copies, and for any
other information, should be addressed to the publisher:
Persea Books, Inc.
171 Madison Avenue
New York, New York 10016

Library of Congress Cataloging-in-Publication Data

The eloquent essay : an anthology of classic and creative
nonfiction from the twentieth century / edited, with an
introduction by John Loughery.
190   p. cm.
Collection of essays originally published 1931–1998.
"A Karen and Michael Braziller Book."

ISBN 0-89255-241-7 (alk. paper)
1. American essays—20th century. 2. English essays—20th
century. I. Loughery, John.
PS688 .E48 1999
814'.508—dc21   99-13309
                                                              CIP

Designed by Leah Lococo
Typeset in Adobe Garamond by Keystrokes, Lenox, Massachusetts

First Edition

Contents

THE DEATH OF THE NOVEL, a shrinking audience for poetry, the decline of ambitious writing for the stage, great oratory replaced by sound bites: whether accepted as fact or speculated upon as a worrisome trend, the common view of the literary arts in our time is fairly bleak. No doubt, some exaggeration is at work here. For every *Nicholas Nickleby* or *Hedda Gabler,* nineteenth-century readers or audiences suffered through hundreds of lackluster novels and plays; to many people, poetry has always seemed an esoteric art form; and long before Abraham Lincoln took the podium at Gettysburg, Americans were bemoaning the lack of well-wrought public prose from their leaders. Interestingly, though, the essay has never had a fallow or slack period, never known a time when consideration of past masters silenced younger voices or led anyone to conclude that the best days of the genre had come and gone. Even today, when computer and visual literacy present new challenges to print literacy, essays continue to find enthusiastic, even passionate audiences. Why should this be the case?

Its origins and development are telling. The essay in English hit its stride as one of the most dynamic and motley of literary forms. The stateliness of Francis Bacon, the intimate voice of Abraham Cowley, and the high moral tone of Samuel Johnson notwithstanding, British essayists before the Victorians were an aggressive lot. They bring to mind taverns, coffeehouses, drawing rooms, theater lobbies, and town squares—sites of animated conversation, robust spectacle, and acrimonious debate—more than libraries and quiet parlors. James Addison and Richard Steele were urban journalists first and foremost, and in pioneering the periodical essay in the early eighteenth century, they pushed the whole genre beyond the serene, tentative, or purely philosophical parameters of Bacon's imitators. The writer-editors of *The Tatler* and *The Spectator* announced their wish to take aim at "the Folly, extravagance, and Caprice [of British society] . . . [at] every absurd fashion, ridiculous Custom, or affected Form of Speech that makes its Appearance in the world." And so they did, to the delight of England's burgeoning middle-class readership, in lively prose that mixed anecdote and observation, frank commentary and withering satire. In their pamphlets and broadsides as well as their fiction and poetry, Daniel Defoe, Jonathan Swift, Alexander Pope, Henry Fielding, and Oliver Goldsmith contributed equally tart reflections on the manners and mores of the time.

Strong opinion, a relish for comic detail, a sometimes misanthropic veneer, and an implicit faith in the value of public discourse were hallmarks of the English essay in its early years. The last quality on that list is an especially significant one. "People are possest with wrong Notions of Things," the author of *Robinson Crusoe* complained when starting his own political journal in 1704, and it clearly followed from that sentiment that the commentator's first duty was to shed light among the uninformed, or at least to attack ignorance without mercy. Yet a keen sense of audience motivated the wiser essayists—they understood the need to instruct by means of wit, irony, paradox, hyperbole, and metaphor, and an ample distance has always separated the treatise from the essay. Arguing the cannibalism of Irish babies to solve the problem of Hibernian overpopulation (Swift's "A Modest Proposal"), urging the execution of religious nonconformists because they might encourage free-thinking among generations yet unborn (Defoe's "The Shortest Way with the Dissenters"), or adopting the persona of an Asian visitor incredulous at the strange ways of Europeans (Goldsmith's "Chinese Letters") were only so many clever strategies toward that wider goal.

By the time Charles Lamb and William Hazlitt captured the imagination of the reading public in the 1820s, devotées of the essay were well prepared for an idiosyncratic voice, a clever narrative line, and self-deprecating asides—in short, for the mixture of artifice and sincerity at the service of intellect that characterizes *Essays of Elia* and *Table Talk*. Indeed, a "feel" for the man—or the woman—behind the words, or for a specific temperament *perceived* to be behind the words, was often as important as the value of the ideas under discussion. Fans of *Letters for Literary Ladies* (1795) reveled in Maria Edgeworth's elegant sarcasm even when they were less comfortable with her veiled feminism. Sometimes the more extravagant the temperament, the better, as Oscar Wilde, Max Beerbohm, Dorothy Parker, and H. L. Mencken were to prove in their different ways. In nineteenth-century America, the situation was the same, as the number of monthlies grew and essayists like Henry David Thoreau, Ralph Waldo Emerson, and Margaret Fuller brought a peculiarly New World, anti-Johnsonian edge to both the personal and the formal essay. Major intellectuals of the day—for example, Thomas Macaulay, Thomas Carlyle, Matthew Arnold, John Ruskin, George Eliot—addressed the weighty historical and aesthetic questions of Victorian life and fueled an unprecedented market for serious analytical prose in Europe and the United States.

Readers of the English and American essay have also been accustomed from the outset to an elasticity of form that has the advantage of appealing to a world of different tastes. The essay as a letter, review, story, appreciation, parody, portrait, travelogue, reminiscence, diatribe, dialogue, oration, dissection, debate, or as the seemingly ingenuous act of thinking aloud piques every literate person's curiosity at some time or other. Twentieth-century writers as varied as Mary McCarthy, Edmund Wilson, E. B. White, James Baldwin, Gore Vidal,

Carlos Fuentes, Bruce Chatwin, Richard Rodriguez, Adrienne Rich, and Gloria Anzaldua have, by means of style and structure as much as theme and outlook, continued to enlarge the audience for the essay. Of equal significance, the essay in English has lasted—and flourished—because it has been able to accommodate itself to a range of topics almost unthinkable in fiction, drama, biography, or autobiography. The struggle for power, apocalyptic evil, private tragedy, romantic love, moral growth, and the family romance: these are the staple subjects of all literature and will be for as long as human beings care to ponder the meaning of their lives and the social bonds they forge. But the pleasure of wasting time, the death throes of a moth, or the gravity and whimsy of the semicolon can occupy pages upon pages in the hands of Robert Louis Stevenson, Virginia Woolf, or Nicholson Baker. Observation and sensation themselves become pressing themes for the skillful essayist, who, relieved of the dictates of plot, enters into a pact with his reader to amuse, provoke, and educate by any means necessary. The multicultural debates of the late twentieth century have likewise added not only new perspectives to Western cultural criticism about subjects previously overlooked but new strategies for communication across boundaries and the evocation of personal truths.

The selection of essays in this anthology is designed to suggest the vitality of a living tradition, to acknowledge the breadth of interests that continues to engage modern essayists, some of whom are the literary ancestors of Defoe, Addison, Steele, Hazlitt, Thoreau, and Woolf. Their subject matter ranges from the largest issues that can confront any society—racial injustice (Martin Luther King, Jr.'s "Letter from a Birmingham Jail"), incomprehensible violence (Bruno Bettelheim's "The Ignored Lesson of Anne Frank"), the destruction of the environment and man's relationship to wildlife (Edward Abbey's "The Cowboy and His Cow" and Ann S. Causey's "Is Hunting Ethical?")—to more literary topics, such as Eudora Welty's reflections on her craft in "Writing and Analyzing a Short Story" and the controversies over *The Adventures of Huckleberry Finn* in Leo Marx's "Huck at 100." Carl Sagan and Pico Iyer ask their readers to tend to the tools of communication themselves. The comma is a gift from the gods, Iyer lyrically suggests (in "In Praise of the Humble Comma"), but the manipulation of words is a skill that threatens to give the crafty and unscrupulous among us an unfair advantage, as Sagan warns in his instructional guide, "The Fine Art of Baloney Detection."

The writers in this collection—crafty but not unscrupulous—take advantage of their readers in eminently fair ways. They write out of passion and conviction or the honest urge to raise questions they cannot resolve, but they write with a keen sense of the strategies at their disposal. Their essays illustrate the abundant variety of forms that have evolved in a genre that has often been makeshift, untidy, resistant to academic rules and definitions. At first glance, for instance, George Orwell's "A Hanging" (1939) and Ellen Ullman's "Space Is Numeric" (1995) would appear to be examples of short fiction: they read like stories with an identifiable setting, characters, developing actions, and plausible resolutions. Yet both authors knew what they were about when they acknowledged their work as anecdotal essays. The rigorous arguments they conduct—in the one instance, about capital punishment, and in the other, about the power of technology to help and ultimately to govern our lives—are securely within the province of a modern understanding of the essay. An anecdotal essay, Orwell and Ullman remind us, is no less a debate about a vital issue because it provokes our thoughts by means of a narrative voice, subtle description, and a lean but compelling plot.

W. H. Auden's "The Guilty Vicarage" offers a model of a

segmented essay, breaking down the constituent parts of his addiction—detective stories—to better understand the whole. His mini-chapter headings (for instance, "Why Murder?" "The Victim," "The Murderer," "The Suspects") can be read as a droll parody of the process of dissection at the same time that they do, in fact, shed light on a pastime that has (in Auden's words) an essentially "magical function." Dr. King's "Letter from a Birmingham Jail" is an example of an "open letter," a missive ostensibly directed to a few individuals but really intended for the world—and intended to have an aura, and a relationship with its audience, vastly different from that of an editorial or a speech. Joan Didion's profile of the artist Georgia O'Keeffe functions on different levels as well: as a portrait of an individual, a subtler portrait of the writer in the act of viewing that individual, and a meditation on the complex ways in which men and women perceive each other and realize their ambitions. A portrait for Didion is a springboard to a consideration of a host of other interesting topics that, properly done, never loses sight of its original focus.

Some subjects are more convincingly probed through the lens of history, in the manner of Bruno Bettelheim in "The Ignored Lesson of Anne Frank" and Lewis Thomas in "Becoming a Doctor." Bettelheim questions the common but unfortunate tendency of people to cling to outmoded "symbols of security" in the face of anxiety and evil. Writing fifteen years after the end of the Second World War, he locates a paradigm of that dilemma in the experience of the Frank family and other victims of Nazi terror. Thomas ponders the nature of the profession he has chosen—as well as its uncertain future and the expectations it has raised—in the context of its development from the nineteenth century to the 1990s.

A few of the writers in the collection make no bones about their position as social critics, adversaries to dominant trends or the powers-that-be. For Edward Abbey, full of opinions about the beef industry and grazing practices in the West, that stance takes the form of an intentionally inflammatory oration in "The Cowboy and His Cow," complete with parenthetical, angry audience responses. For I. F. Stone, a fresh review of Socrates' trial and the always-relevant issue of the censorship of unpopular ideas is best expressed by means of a Socratic dialogue—with the writer of "When Free Speech Was First Condemned" artfully providing the questions and the answers himself. In a more practical (but still imaginative) vein, Carl Sagan gives his readers a comprehensive "toolkit," as he calls it, for the detection of "proved or presumptive baloney." Individuals and societies lose their capacity for critical thinking when they are taken in by the "baloney" of bad logic and empty rhetoric: Sagan's lists in "The Fine Art of Baloney Detection" are intended as media antidotes, "baloney kits" to help us separate truth from falsity and propaganda.

Ann S. Causey, Barbara Kingsolver, Amy Tan, and Opal Palmer Adisa approach important public issues in still other ways, electing different routes from the straightforward argumentation of Edward Abbey or Leo Marx. Causey's title sets the stage for a classic debate with a direct proposition ("Is Hunting Ethical?") and does indeed consider both sides of this fiercely argued topic, though she ends by asking a much larger question about the nature of the original query itself. In "How Mr. Dewey Decimal Saved My Life," Kingsolver is more roundabout. What begins as a portrait of smalltown life in Kentucky, adolescent rebellion, and a helpful librarian becomes a sharply digressive essay, leading us on in its last pages to the dangers of "protecting" innocent young readers. Amy Tan in "Mother Tongue" and Opal Palmer Adisa in "Lying in the Tall Grasses, Eating Cane" exploit the qualities of personal narrative to good effect. Tan describes in humorous detail her relationship with her immigrant mother, a speaker of "broken English," even as she considers the ways in which prejudice about language defines us all. Adisa recollects a Jamaican childhood in the open air, a British education that denied her a cultural heritage, a yearning to write: one individual's history, both dynamic and poignant, that nonetheless steers its readers toward universal themes—of self-assertion and racial identity, of voices painstakingly found.

Finally, Pico Iyer demonstrates the modern essayist's ability to explore, even extol, the smallest subjects through the techniques of association, example, embellishment, and minute, loving examination. "In Praise of the Humble Comma" fulfills its purpose in a cascade of metaphor (has the comma ever been compared to so many other signs, objects, states of nature, and types of people?), variously punctuated sentences, and lists of poetic and practical ends to which this simple mark of punctuation might be put. Iyer's is the voice of the inspired lover or devout worshipper—itself an approach, a strategy, that is hard to resist.

"The secret of writing a good essay," J. B. Priestley once noted, "is to let yourself go." To be sure, Priestley wasn't arguing the virtues of formlessness or self-indulgence. But he was speaking of the need to look beyond prepackaged ideas and ready-made structures. He was alluding to the rough-and-tumble, ad hoc origins of the essay. An essay that does justice to its subject but ultimately transcends that subject and the customary ways of perceiving it, that compels us to consider *how* meaning is conveyed as well as *what* that meaning is, situates itself closer to the reality of how we actually think, remember, form associations, question, argue, and learn. For the writers in this collection, that goal is all-important, and the lines between storytelling and formal essay-writing, memoir and exposition, sensual delight and intellectual rigor, the demotic and the man-darin, are appropriately blurred.

That kind of protean force calls for an equivalent openness and flexibility on the part of the reader. To extend Priestley's idea: the secret of reading a good essay is also "to let yourself go," to trust to the writer's sense of mission and eloquence, and the readers of this book are invited to do just that.

JOHN LOUGHERY
October 1999

For a thorough discussion of the essays and how they can be used in the class-room, please request a free teacher's guide by John Loughery. Contact Persea Books, 171 Madison Avenue, New York, New York 10016; telephone (212) 779-7668; fax (212) 689-5405; e-mail PerseaBks@aol.com.

The

ELOQUENT
ESSAY

George Orwell

A HANGING
1931

Though best known for his postwar political fiction, *Animal Farm* and *Nineteen Eighty-four,* George Orwell (born Eric Blair) had produced an impressive body of work even before the Second World War. His famous study of the Spanish Civil War, *Homage to Catalonia* (1938), is a classic example of modern political reportage. *Down and Out in Paris and London* (1933) narrated the author's days spent among the working-class poor of Europe, while *The Road to Wigan Pier* (1937) analyzed the Socialist response to Depression-era poverty. His novels *A Clergyman's Daughter* (1935) and *Keep the Aspidistra Flying* (1936) were perceptive studies of English life. Like *Animal Farm* and *Nineteen Eighty-Four,* Orwell's writings about his experiences serving the colonial government in British-occupied Burma—especially the novel *Burmese Days* (1934) and the essays "Shooting an Elephant" and "A Hanging"—explore the nature of power and subjugation, government authority and personal responsibility, duty and morality.

IT WAS IN BURMA, a sodden morning of the rains. A sickly light, like yellow tinfoil, was slanting over the high walls into the jail yard. We were waiting outside the condemned cells, a row of sheds fronted with double bars, like small animal cages. Each cell measured about ten feet by ten and was quite bare within except for a plank bed and a pot for drinking water. In some of them brown silent men were squatting at the inner bars, with their blankets draped round them. These were the condemned men due to be hanged within the next week or two.

One prisoner had been brought out of his cell. He was a Hindu, a puny wisp of a man, with a shaven head and vague liquid eyes. He had a thick, sprouting moustache, absurdly too big for his body, rather like the moustache of a comic man on the films. Six tall Indian warders were guarding him and getting him ready for the gallows. Two of them stood by with rifles and fixed bayonets, while the others handcuffed him, passed a chain through his handcuffs and fixed it to their belts, and lashed his arms tight to his sides. They crowded very close about him, with their hands always on him in a careful, caressing grip as though all the while feeling him to make sure he was there. It was like men handling a fish which is still alive and may jump back into the water. But he stood quite unresisting, yielding his arms limply to the ropes, as though he hardly noticed what was happening.

Eight o'clock struck and a bugle call, desolately thin in the wet air, floated from the distant barracks. The superintendent of the jail, who was standing apart from the rest of us, moodily prodding the gravel with his stick, raised his head at the sound. He was an army doctor, with a gray toothbrush moustache and a gruff voice. "For God's sake hurry up, Francis," he said irritably. "The man ought to have been dead by this time. Aren't you ready yet?"

Francis, the head jailer, a fat Dravidian in a white drill suit and gold spectacles, waved his black hand. "Yes sir, yes sir," he bubbled. "All iss satisfactorily prepared. The hangman iss waiting. We shall proceed."

"Well, quick march, then. The prisoners can't get their breakfast till this job's over."

We set out for the gallows. Two warders marched on either side of the prisoner, with their rifles at the slope; two others marched close against him, gripping him by arm and shoulder, as though at once pushing and supporting him. The rest of us, magistrates and the like, followed behind. Suddenly, when we had gone ten yards, the procession stopped short without any order or warning. A dreadful thing had happened—a dog, come goodness knows whence, had appeared in the yard. It came bounding among us with a loud volley of barks, and leapt round us wagging its whole body, wild with glee at finding so many human beings together. It was a large woolly dog, half Airedale, half pariah. For a moment it pranced round us, and then, before anyone could stop it, it had made a dash for the prisoner and, jumping up, tried to lick his face. Everyone stood aghast, too taken aback even to grab at the dog.

"Who let that bloody brute in here?" said the superintendent angrily. "Catch it, someone!"

A warder, detached from the escort, charged clumsily after the dog, but it danced and gamboled just out of his reach, taking everything as part of the game. A young Eurasian jailer picked up a handful of gravel and tried to stone the dog away, but it dodged the stones and came after us again. Its yaps echoed from the jail walls. The prisoner, in the grasp of the two warders, looked on incuriously, as though this was another formality of the hanging. It was several minutes before someone managed to catch the dog. Then we put my handkerchief through its collar and moved off once more, with the dog still straining and whimpering.

It was about forty yards to the gallows. I watched the bare brown back of the prisoner marching in front of me. He walked clumsily with his bound arms, but quite steadily, with that bobbing gait of the Indian who never straightens his knees. At each step his muscles slid neatly into place, the lock of hair on his scalp danced up and down, his feet printed themselves on the wet gravel. And once, in spite of the men who gripped him by each shoulder, he stepped slightly aside to avoid a puddle on the path.

It is curious, but till that moment I had never realized what it means to destroy a healthy, conscious man. When I saw the prisoner step aside to avoid the puddle I saw the mystery, the unspeakable wrongness, of cutting a life short when it is in full tide. This man was not dying, he was alive just as we are alive. All the organs of his body were working—bowels digesting food, skin renewing itself, nails growing, tissues forming—all toiling away in solemn foolery. His nails would still be growing when he stood on the drop, when he was falling through the air with a tenth of a second to live. His eyes saw the yellow gravel and the gray walls, and his brain still remembered, foresaw, reasoned—reasoned even about puddles. He and we were a party of men walking together, seeing, hearing, feeling, understanding the same world: and in two minutes, with a sudden snap, one of us would be gone—one mind less, one world less.

The gallows stood in a small yard, separate from the main grounds of the prison, and overgrown with tall prickly weeds. It was a brick erection like three sides of a shed, with planking on top, and above that two beams and a crossbar with the rope dangling. The hangman, a gray-haired convict in the white uniform of the prison, was waiting beside his machine. He greeted us with a servile crouch as we entered. At a word from Francis the two warders, gripping the prisoner more closely than ever, half led, half pushed him to the gallows and helped him clumsily up the ladder. Then the hangman climbed up and fixed the rope round the prisoner's neck.

We stood waiting, five yards away. The warders had formed in a rough circle round the gallows. And then, when the noose was fixed, the prisoner began crying out to his god. It was a high, reiterated cry of "Ram! Ram! Ram! Ram!" not urgent and fearful like a prayer or cry for help, but steady, rhythmical, almost like the tolling of a bell. The dog answered the sound with a whine. The hangman, still standing on the gallows, produced a small cotton bag like a flour bag and drew it down over the prisoner's face. But the sound, muffled by the cloth, still persisted, over and over again: "Ram! Ram! Ram! Ram! Ram!"

The hangman climbed down and stood ready, holding the

lever. Minutes seemed to pass. The steady, muffled crying from the prisoner went on and on, "Ram! Ram! Ram!" never faltering for an instant. The superintendent, his head on his chest, was slowly poking the ground with his stick; perhaps he was counting the cries, allowing the prisoner a fixed number—fifty, perhaps, or a hundred. Everyone had changed color. The Indians had gone gray like bad coffee, and one or two of the bayonets were wavering. We looked at the lashed, hooded man on the drop, and listened to his cries—each cry another second of life; the same thought was in all our minds: oh, kill him quickly, get it over, stop that abominable noise!

Suddenly the superintendent made up his mind. Throwing up his head he made a swift motion with his stick. "Chalo!" he shouted almost fiercely.

There was a clanking noise, and then dead silence. The prisoner had vanished, and the rope was twisting on itself. I let go of the dog, and it galloped immediately to the back of the gallows; but when it got there it stopped short, barked, and then retreated into a corner of the yard, where it stood among the weeds, looking timorously out at us. We went round the gallows to inspect the prisoner's body. He was dangling with his toes pointed straight downward, very slowly revolving, as dead as a stone.

The superintendent reached out with his stick and poked the bare brown body; it oscillated slightly. "*He's* all right," said the superintendent. He backed out from under the gallows, and blew out a deep breath. The moody look had gone out of his face quite suddenly. He glanced at his wrist watch. "Eight minutes past eight. Well, that's all for this morning, thank God."

The warders unfixed bayonets and marched away. The dog, sobered and conscious of having misbehaved itself, slipped after them. We walked out of the gallows yard, past the condemned cells with their waiting prisoners, into the big central yard of the prison. The convicts, under the command of warders armed with lathis, were already receiving their breakfast. They squatted in long rows, each man holding a tin pannikin, while two warders with buckets marched round ladling out rice; it seemed quite a homely, jolly scene, after the hanging. An enormous relief had come upon us now that the job was done. One felt an impulse to sing, to break into a run, to snigger. All at once everyone began chattering gaily.

The Eurasian boy walking beside me nodded toward the way we had come, with a knowing smile: "Do you know, sir, our friend [he meant the dead man] when he heard his appeal had been dismissed, he pissed on the floor of his cell. From fright. Kindly take one of my cigarettes, sir. Do you not admire my new silver case, sir? From the boxwalah, two rupees eight annas. Classy European style."

Several people laughed—at what, nobody seemed certain.

Francis was walking by the superintendent, talking garrulously: "Well, sir, all hass passed off with the utmost satisfactoriness. It was all finished—flick! like that. It iss not always so—oah, no! I have known cases where the doctor wass obliged to go beneath the gallows and pull the prissoner's legs to ensure decease. Most disagreeable!"

"Wriggling about, eh? That's bad," said the superintendent.

"Ach, sir, it iss worse when they become refractory! One man, I recall, clung to the bars of hiss cage when we went to take him out. You will scarcely credit, sir, that it took six warders to dislodge him, three pulling at each leg. We reasoned with him. 'My dear fellow,' we said, 'think of all the pain and trouble you are causing to us!' But no, he would not listen! Ach, he wass very troublesome!"

I found that I was laughing quite loudly. Everyone was laughing. Even the superintendent grinned in a tolerant way. "You'd better all come out and have a drink," he said quite genially. "I've got a bottle of whisky in the car. We could do with it."

We went through the big double gates of the prison into the road. "Pulling at his legs!" exclaimed a Burmese magistrate suddenly, and burst into a loud chuckling. We all began laughing again. At that moment Francis' anecdote seemed extraordinarily funny. We all had a drink together, native and European alike, quite amicably. The dead man was a hundred yards away.

W. H. Auden

THE GUILTY VICARAGE
1948

Born in England in 1907 and educated at Oxford, W. H. Auden was, by the age of thirty, one of the most admired poets writing in the English language. During the late 1920s and 1930s, he traveled extensively—to Weimar Germany, Iceland, China, and Spain during the Spanish Civil War—published several collections of poetry, and collaborated on musical compositions and plays with Benjamin Britten and Christopher Isherwood respectively. In 1939 Auden emigrated with Isherwood to the United States and became an American citizen in 1946. Though best known for his lyric poetry, Auden also published hundreds of book reviews and dozens of critical essays in his forty-year career and, as editor of the Yale Series of Young Poets from 1947 to 1962, supported the work of fledgling writers. He was respected as a man of perceptive judgments and wide-ranging literary tastes.

I had not known sin, but by the law.

ROMANS VII,7

A CONFESSION

FOR ME, AS FOR MANY OTHERS, the reading of detective stories is an addiction like tobacco or alcohol. The symptoms of this are: firstly, the intensity of the craving—if I have any work to do, I must be careful not to get hold of a detective story for, once I begin one, I cannot work or sleep till I have finished it. Secondly, its specificity—the story must conform to certain formulas (I find it very difficult, for example, to read one that is not set in rural England). And, thirdly, its immediacy. I forget the story as soon as I have finished it, and have no wish to read it again. If, as sometimes happens, I start reading one and find after a few pages that I have read it before, I cannot go on.

Such reactions convince me that, in my case at least, detective stories have nothing to do with works of art. It is possible, however, that an analysis of the detective story, i.e., of the kind of detective story I enjoy, may throw light, not only on its magical function, but also, by contrast, on the function of art.

DEFINITION

The vulgar definition, "a Whodunit," is correct. The basic formula is this: a murder occurs; many are suspected; all but one suspect, who is the murderer, are eliminated; the murderer is arrested or dies.

This definition excludes:

1) Studies of murderers whose guilt is known, e.g., *Malice Aforethought.* There are borderline cases in which the murderer is known and there are no false suspects, but the proof is lacking, e.g., many of the stories of Freeman Wills Crofts. Most of these are permissible.

2) Thrillers, spy stories, stories of master crooks, etc., when the identification of the criminal is subordinate to the defeat of his criminal designs.

The interest in the thriller is the ethical and characteristic conflict between good and evil, between Us and Them. The interest in the study of a murderer is the observation, by the innocent many, of the sufferings of the guilty one. The interest in the detective story is the dialectic of innocence and guilt.

As in the Aristotelian description of tragedy, there is Concealment (the innocent seem guilty and the guilty seem innocent) and Manifestation (the real guilt is brought to consciousness). There is also peripeteia, in this case not a reversal of fortune but a double reversal from apparent guilt to innocence and from apparent innocence to guilt. The formula may be diagrammed as follows:

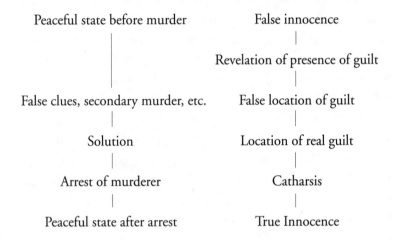

Peaceful state before murder

False clues, secondary murder, etc.

Solution

Arrest of murderer

Peaceful state after arrest

False innocence

Revelation of presence of guilt

False location of guilt

Location of real guilt

Catharsis

True Innocence

In Greek tragedy the audience knows the truth; the actors do not, but discover or bring to pass the inevitable. In modern, e.g., Elizabethan, tragedy the audience knows neither less nor more than the most knowing of the actors. In the detective story the audience does not know the truth at all; one of the actors— the murderer—does; and the detective, of his own free will, discovers and reveals what the murderer, of his own free will, tries to conceal.

Greek tragedy and the detective story have one characteristic in common in which they both differ from modern tragedy, namely, the characters are not changed in or by their actions: in Greek tragedy because their actions are fated, in the detective story because the decisive event, the murder, has already occurred. Time and space therefore are simply the when and where of revealing either what has to happen or what has actually happened. In consequence, the detective story probably should, and usually does, obey the classical unities, whereas modern tragedy, in which the characters develop with time, can only do so by a technical tour de force; and the thriller, like the picaresque novel, even demands frequent changes of time and place.

WHY MURDER?

There are three classes of crime: (A) offenses against God and one's neighbor or neighbors; (B) offenses against God and society; (C) offenses against God. (All crimes, of course, are offenses against oneself.)

Murder is a member and the only member of Class B. The character common to all crimes in Class A is that it is possible, at least theoretically, either that restitution can be made to the injured party (e.g., stolen goods can be returned), or that the injured party can forgive the criminal (e.g., in the case of rape). Consequently, society as a whole is only indirectly involved; its representatives (the police, etc.) act in the interests of the injured party.

Murder is unique in that it abolishes the party it injures, so that society has to take the place of the victim and on his behalf demand restitution or grant forgiveness; it is the one crime in which society has a direct interest.

Many detective stories begin with a death that appears to be suicide and is later discovered to have been murder. Suicide is a crime belonging to Class C in which neither the criminal's neighbors nor society has any interest, direct or indirect. As long as a death is believed to be suicide, even private curiosity is improper; as soon as it is proved to be murder, public inquiry becomes a duty.

The detective story has five elements—the milieu, the victim, the murderer, the suspects, the detectives.

THE MILIEU (HUMAN)

The detective story requires:

1) A closed society so that the possibility of an outside murderer (and hence of the society being totally innocent) is excluded; and a closely related society so that all its members are potentially suspect (*cf.* the thriller, which requires an open society in which any stranger may be a friend or enemy in disguise).

Such conditions are met by: a) the group of blood relatives (the Christmas dinner in the country house); b) the closely knit geographical group (the old world village); c) the occupational group (the theatrical company); d) the group isolated by the neutral place (the Pullman car).

In this last type the concealment-manifestation formula applies not only to the murder but also to the relations between the members of the group who first appear to be strangers to each other, but are later found to be related.

2) It must appear to be an innocent society in a state of grace, i.e., a society where there is no need of the law, no contradiction between the aesthetic individual and the ethical universal, and where murder, therefore, is the unheard-of act which precipitates a crisis (for it reveals that some member has fallen and is no longer in a state of grace). The law becomes a reality and for a time all must live in its shadow, till the fallen one is identified. With his arrest, innocence is restored, and the law retires forever.

The characters in a detective story should, therefore, be eccentric (aesthetically interesting individuals) and good (instinctively ethical)—good, that is, either in appearance, later shown to be false, or in reality, first concealed by an appearance of bad.

It is a sound instinct that has made so many detective story writers choose a college as a setting. The ruling passion of the ideal professor is the pursuit of knowledge for its own sake so that he is related to other human beings only indirectly through their common relation to the truth; and those passions, like lust and avarice and envy, which relate individuals directly and may lead to murder are, in his case, ideally excluded. If a murder occurs in a college, therefore, it is a sign that some colleague is not only a bad man but also a bad professor. Further, as the basic premise of academic life is that truth is universal and to be shared with all, the *gnosis* of a concrete crime and the *gnosis* of abstract ideas nicely parallel and parody each other.

(The even more ideal contradiction of a murder in a monastery is excluded by the fact that monks go regularly to confession and, while the murderer might well not confess his crime, the suspects who are innocent of murder but guilty of lesser sins cannot be supposed to conceal them without making the monastery absurd. Incidentally, is it an accident that the detective story has flourished most in predominantly Protestant countries?)

The detective story writer is also wise to choose a society with an elaborate ritual and to describe this in detail. A ritual is a sign of harmony between the aesthetic and the ethical in which body and mind, individual will and general laws, are not in conflict. The murderer uses his knowledge of the ritual to commit the crime and can be caught only by someone who acquires an equal or superior familiarity with it.

THE MILIEU (NATURAL)

In the detective story, as in its mirror image, the Quest for the Grail, maps (the ritual of space) and timetables (the ritual of time) are desirable. Nature should reflect its human inhabitants, i.e., it should be the Great Good Place; for the more Eden-like it is, the greater the contradiction of murder. The country is preferable to the town, a well-to-do neighborhood (but not too well-to-do—or there will be a suspicion of ill-gotten gains) better than a slum. The corpse must shock not only because it is a corpse but also because, even for a corpse, it is shockingly out of place, as when a dog makes a mess on a drawing room carpet.

Mr. Raymond Chandler has written that he intends to take the body out of the vicarage garden and give the murder back to those who are good at it. If he wishes to write detective stories, i.e., stories where the reader's principal interest is to learn who did it, he could not be more mistaken, for in a society of professional criminals, the only possible motives for desiring to identify the murderer are blackmail or revenge, which both apply to individuals, not to the group as a whole, and can equally well inspire murder. Actually, whatever he may say, I think Mr. Chandler is interested in writing, not detective stories, but serious studies of a criminal milieu, the Great Wrong Place, and his powerful but extremely depressing books should be read and judged, not as escape literature, but as works of art.

THE VICTIM

The victim has to try to satisfy two contradictory requirements. He has to involve everyone in suspicion, which requires that he be a bad character; and he has to make everyone feel guilty, which requires that he be a good character. He cannot be a criminal because he could then be dealt with by the law and murder would be unnecessary. (Blackmail is the only exception.) The more general the temptation to murder he arouses, the better; e.g., the desire for freedom is a better motive than money alone or sex alone. On the whole, the best victim is the negative Father or Mother Image.

If there is more than one murder, the subsequent victims should be more innocent than the initial victim, i.e., the murderer should start with a real grievance and, as a consequence of righting it by illegitimate means, be forced to murder against his will where he has no grievances but his own guilt.

THE MURDERER

Murder is negative creation, and every murderer is therefore the rebel who claims the right to be omnipotent. His pathos is his refusal to suffer. The problem for the writer is to conceal his demonic pride from the other characters and from the reader, since, if a person has this pride, it tends to appear in everything he says and does. To surprise the reader when the identity of the murderer is revealed, yet at the same time to convince him that everything he has previously been told about the murderer is consistent with his being a murderer, is the test of a good detective story.

As to the murderer's end, of the three alternatives—execution, suicide, and madness—the first is preferable; for if he commits suicide he refuses to repent, and if he goes mad he cannot repent, but if he does not repent society cannot forgive. Execution on the other hand, is the act of atonement by which the murderer is forgiven by society. In real life I disapprove of capital punishment, but in a detective story the murderer must have no future.

(*A Suggestion for Mr. Chandler:* Among a group of efficient professional killers who murder for strictly professional reasons, there is one to whom, like Leopold and Loeb, murder is an *acte gratuite.* Presently murders begin to occur which have not been commissioned. The group is morally outraged and bewildered; it has to call in the police to detect the amateur murderer, rescue the professionals from a mutual suspicion which threatens to disrupt their organization, and restore their capacity to murder.)

THE SUSPECTS

The detective-story society is a society consisting of apparently innocent individuals, i.e., their aesthetic interest as individuals does not conflict with their ethical obligations to the universal. The murder is the act of disruption by which innocence is lost, and the individual and the law become opposed to each other. In the case of the murderer this opposition is completely real (till he is arrested and consents to be punished); in the case of the suspects it is mostly apparent.

But in order for the appearance to exist, there must be some element of reality; e.g., it is unsatisfactory if the suspicion is caused by chance or the murderer's malice alone. The suspects must be guilty of something, because, now that the aesthetic and the ethical are in opposition, if they are completely innocent (obedient to the ethical) they lose their aesthetic interest and the reader will ignore them.

For suspects, the principal causes of guilt are:

1) the wish or even the intention to murder;

2) crimes of Class A or vices of Class C (e.g., illicit amours) which the suspect is afraid or ashamed to reveal;

3) a *hubris* of intellect which tries to solve the crime itself and despises the official police (assertion of the supremacy of the aesthetic over the ethical). If great enough, this *hubris* leads to its subject getting murdered;

4) a *hubris* of innocence which refuses to cooperate with the investigation;

5) a lack of faith in another loved suspect, which leads its subject to hide or confuse clues.

THE DETECTIVE

Completely satisfactory detectives are extremely rare. Indeed, I only know of three: Sherlock Holmes (Conan Doyle), Inspector French (Freeman Wills Crofts), and Father Brown (Chesterton).

The job of detective is to restore the state of grace in which the aesthetic and the ethical are as one. Since the murderer who caused their disjunction is the aesthetically defiant individual, his opponent, the detective, must be either the official representative of the ethical or the exceptional individual who is himself in a state of grace. If he is the former, he is a professional; if he is the latter, he is an amateur. In either case, the detective must be the total stranger who cannot possibly be involved in the crime; this excludes the local police and should, I think, exclude the detective who is a friend of one of the suspects. The professional detective has the advantage that, since he is not an individual but a representative of the ethical, he does not need a motive for investigating the crime; but for the same reason he has the disadvantage of being unable to overlook the minor ethical violations of the suspects, and therefore it is harder for him to gain their confidence.

Most amateur detectives, on the other hand, are unsatisfactory either because they are priggish supermen, like Lord Peter Wimsey and Philo Vance, who have no motive for being detectives except caprice, or because, like the detectives of the hard-boiled school, they are motivated by avarice or ambition and might just as well be murderers.

The amateur detective genius may have weaknesses to give him aesthetic interest, but they must not be of a kind which outrage ethics. The most satisfactory weaknesses are the solitary oral vices of eating and drinking or childish boasting. In his sexual life, the detective must be either celibate or happily married.

Between the amateur detective and the professional policeman stands the criminal lawyer whose *telos* is, not to discover who is guilty, but to prove that his client is innocent. His ethical justification is that human law is ethically imperfect, i.e., not an absolute manifestation of the universal and divine, and subject to chance aesthetic limitations, e.g., the intelligence or stupidity of individual policemen and juries (in consequence of which an innocent man may sometimes be judged guilty).

To correct this imperfection, the decision is arrived at through an aesthetic combat, i.e., the intellectual gifts of the defense versus those of the prosecution, just as in earlier days doubtful cases were solved by physical combat between the accused and the accuser.

The lawyer-detective (e.g., Joshua Clunk) is never quite satisfactory, therefore, because of his commitment to his client, whom he cannot desert, even if he should really be the guilty party, without ceasing to be a lawyer.

SHERLOCK HOLMES

Holmes is the exceptional individual who is in a state of grace because he is a genius in whom scientific curiosity is raised to the status of a heroic passion. He is erudite but his knowledge is absolutely specialized (e.g., his ignorance of the Copernican system), he is in all matters outside his field as helpless as a child (e.g., his untidiness), and he pays the price for his scientific detachment (his neglect of feeling) by being the victim of melancholia which attacks him whenever he is unoccupied with a case (e.g., his violin playing and cocaine taking).

His motive for being a detective is, positively, a love of the neutral truth (he has no interest in the feelings of the guilty or the innocent), and negatively, a need to escape from his own feelings of melancholy. His attitude towards people and his technique of observation and deduction are those of the chemist or physicist. If he chooses human beings rather than inanimate matter as his material, it is because investigating the inanimate is unheroically easy since it cannot tell lies, which human beings can and do, so that in dealing with them, observation must be twice as sharp and logic twice as rigorous.

INSPECTOR FRENCH

His class and culture are those natural to a Scotland Yard inspector. (The old Oxonian Inspector is insufferable.) His motive is love of duty. Holmes detects for his own sake and shows the maximum indifference to all feelings except a negative fear of his own. French detects for the sake of the innocent members of society, and is indifferent only to his own feelings and those of the murderer. (He would much rather stay at home with his wife.) He is exceptional only in his exceptional love of duty which makes him take exceptional pains; he does only what all could do as well if they had the same patient industry (his checking of alibis for tiny flaws which careless hurry had missed). He outwits the murderer, partly because the latter is not quite so painstaking as he, and partly because the murderer must act alone, while he has the help of all the innocent people in the world who are doing their duty, e.g., the postmen, railway clerks, milkmen, etc., who become, accidentally, witnesses to the truth.

FATHER BROWN

Like Holmes, an amateur; yet, like French, not an individual genius. His activities as a detective are an incidental part of his activities as a priest who cares for souls. His prime motive is compassion, of which the guilty are in greater need than the innocent, and he investigates murders, not for his own sake, nor even for the sake of the innocent, but for the sake of the murderer who can save his soul if he will confess and repent. He solves his cases, not by approaching them objectively like a scientist or a policeman, but by subjectively imagining himself to be the murderer, a process which is good not only for the murderer but for Father Brown himself because, as he says, "it gives a man his remorse beforehand."

Holmes and French can only help the murderer as teachers, i.e., they can teach him that murder will out and does not pay. More they cannot do since neither is tempted to murder; Holmes is too gifted, French too well trained in the habit of virtue. Father Brown can go further and help the murderer as an example, i.e., as a man who is also tempted to murder, but is able by faith to resist temptation.

THE READER

The most curious fact about the detective story is that it makes its greatest appeal precisely to those classes of people who are most immune to other forms of daydream literature. The typical detective story addict is a doctor or clergyman or scientist or artist, i.e., a fairly successful professional man with intellectual interests and well-read in his own field, who could never stomach the *Saturday Evening Post* or *True Confessions* or movie magazines or comics. If I ask myself why I cannot enjoy stories about strong silent men and lovely girls who make love in a beautiful landscape and come into millions of dollars, I cannot answer that I have no fantasies of being handsome and loved and rich, because of course I have (though my life is, perhaps, sufficiently fortunate to make me less envious in a naïve way than some). No, I can only say that I am too conscious of the absurdity of such wishes to enjoy seeing them reflected in print.

I can, to some degree, resist yielding to these or similar desires which tempt me, but I cannot prevent myself from having them to resist; and it is the fact that I have them which makes me feel guilty, so that instead of dreaming about indulging my desires, I dream about the removal of the guilt which I feel at their existence. This I still do, and must do, because guilt is a subjective feeling where any further step is only a reduplication—feeling guilty about guilt. I suspect that the typical reader of detective stories is, like myself, a person who suffers from a sense of sin. From the point of view of ethics, desires and acts are good and bad, and I must choose the good and reject the bad, but the I which makes this choice is ethically neutral; it only becomes good or bad in its choice. To have a sense of sin means to feel guilty at there being an ethical choice to make, a guilt which, however "good" I may become, remains unchanged. It is sometimes said that detective stories are read by respectable law-abiding citizens in order to gratify in fantasy the violent or murderous wishes they dare not, or are ashamed to, translate into action. This may be true for the reader of thrillers (which I rarely enjoy), but it is quite false for the reader of detective stories. On the contrary, the magical satisfaction the latter provide (which makes them escape literature, not works of art) is the illusion of being dissociated from the murderer.

The magic formula is an innocence which is discovered to contain guilt; then a suspicion of being the guilty one; and finally a real innocence from which the guilty other has been expelled, a cure effected, not by me or my neighbors, but by the miraculous intervention of a genius from outside who removes guilt by giving knowledge of guilt. (The detective story subscribes, in fact, to the Socratic daydream: "Sin is ignorance.")

If one thinks of a work of art which deals with murder, *Crime and Punishment* for example, its effect on the reader is to compel an identification with the murderer which he would prefer not to recognize. The identification of fantasy is always an attempt to avoid one's own suffering: the identification of art is a sharing in the suffering of another. Kafka's *The Trial* is another instructive example of the difference between a work of art and the detective story. In the latter it is certain that a crime has been committed and, temporarily, uncertain to whom the guilt should be attached; as soon as this is known, the innocence of everyone else is certain. (Should it turn out that after all no crime has been committed, then all would be innocent.) In *The Trial,* on the other hand, it is the guilt that is certain and the crime that is uncertain; the aim of the hero's investigation is not to prove his innocence (which would be impossible for he knows he is guilty), but to discover what, if anything, he has done to make himself guilty. K, the hero, is, in fact, a portrait of the kind of person who reads detective stories for escape.

The fantasy, then, which the detective story addict indulges is the fantasy of being restored to the Garden of Eden, to a state of innocence, where he may know love as love and not as the law. The driving force behind this daydream is the feeling of guilt, the cause of which is unknown to the dreamer. The fantasy of escape is the same, whether one explains the guilt in Christian, Freudian, or any other terms. One's way of trying to face the reality, on the other hand, will, of course, depend very much on one's creed.

Eudora Welty

WRITING AND ANALYZING
A STORY
1955

A resident of Jackson, Mississippi for her entire life, Eudora
Welty (b. 1908) is the most famous living Southern writer and one of the
most respected American short-story writers of the twentieth century.
Though her novels *The Robber Bridegroom* (1942), *Losing Battles* (1970),
and *The Optimist's Daughter* (1972) enjoyed a measure of critical and popular success, she has focused almost exclusively on the short story, writing
several much-anthologized classics, including "A Worn Path" and "Why I
Live at the P. O." Welty rarely comments on her work and discourages
any biographical attention, but in "Writing and Analyzing a Story," she
departed from that policy to an extent, offering insights into the craft she
has perfected and the personal inspiration behind one story, "No Place for
You, My Love."

~

WRITERS ARE OFTEN ASKED to give their own
analysis of some story they have published. I never
saw, as reader or writer, that a finished story stood
in need of any more from the author: for better or worse, there
the story is. There is also the question of whether or not the
author could provide the sort of analysis asked for. Story writing
and critical analysis are indeed separate gifts, like spelling and
playing the flute, and the same writer proficient in both has
been doubly endowed. But even he can't rise and do both at the
same time.

To me as a story writer, generalizations about writing come
tardily and uneasily, and I would limit them, if I were wise, by
saying that any conclusions I feel confidence in are stuck to the
particular story, part of the animal. The most trustworthy lesson

I've learned from work so far is the simple one that the writing of each story is sure to open up a different prospect and pose a new problem; and that no past story bears recognizably on a new one or gives any promise of help, even if the writing mind had room for help and the wish that it would come. Help offered from outside the frame of the story would be itself an intrusion.

It's hard for me to believe that a writer's stories, taken in their whole, are written in any typical, predictable, systematically developing, or even chronological way—for all that a serious writer's stories are ultimately, to any reader, so clearly identifiable as his. Each story, it seems to me, thrives in the course of being written only as long as it seems to have a life of its own.

Yet it may become clear to a writer in retrospect (or so it did to me, although I may have been simply tardy to see it) that his stories have repeated themselves in shadowy ways, that they have returned and may return in future too—in variations—to certain themes. They may be following, in their own development, some pattern that's been very early laid down. Of course, such a pattern is subjective in nature; it may lie too deep to be consciously recognized until a cycle of stories and the actions of time have raised it to view. All the same, it is a pattern of which a new story is not another copy but a fresh attempt made in its own full-bodied right and out of its own impulse, with its own pressure, and its own needs of fulfillment.

It seems likely that all of one writer's stories do tend to spring from the same source within him. However they differ in theme or approach, however they vary in mood or fluctuate in their strength, their power to reach the mind or heart, all of one writer's stories carry their signature because of the one impulse most characteristic of his own gift—to praise, to love, to call up into view. But then, what countless stories by what countless authors share a common source! For the source of the short story is usually lyrical. And all writers speak from, and speak to, emotions eternally the same in all of us: love, pity, terror do not show favorites or leave any of us out.

The tracking down of a story might do well to start not in the subjective country but in the world itself. What in this world leads back most directly, makes the clearest connection to these emotions? What is the pull on the line? For some outside signal has startled or moved the story-writing mind to complicity: some certain irresistible, alarming (pleasurable or disturbing), magnetic person, place or thing. The outside world and the writer's response to it, the story's quotients, are always different, always differing in the combining; they are always—or so it seems to me—most intimately connected with each other.

This living connection is one that by its nature is not very open to generalization or discoverable by the ordinary scrutinies of analysis. Never mind; for its existence is, for any purpose but that of the working writer, of little importance to the story itself. It is of merely personal importance. But it is of extraordinary, if temporary, use to the writer for the particular story. Keeping this connection close is a writer's testing device along the way, flexible, delicate, precise, a means of guidance. I would rather submit a story to the test of its outside world, to show what it was doing and how it went about it, than to the method of critical analysis which would pick the story up by its heels (as if it had swallowed a button) to examine the writing process as analysis in reverse, as though a story—or any system of feeling—could be more accessible to understanding for being hung upside down.

It is not from criticism but from this world that stories come in the beginning; their origins are living reference plain to the writer's eye, even though to his eye alone. The writer's mind and heart, where all this exterior is continually *becoming* something—the moral, the passionate, the poetic, hence the *shaping* idea—can't be mapped and plotted. (Would this help—any more than a map hung on the wall changes the world?) It's the form it takes when it comes out the other side, of course, that gives a story something unique—its life. The story, in the way it has arrived at what it is on the page, has been something learned, by dint of the story's challenge and the work that rises to meet it—a process as uncharted for the writer as if it had never been attempted before.

Since analysis has to travel backward, the path it goes is an ever-narrowing one, whose goal is the vanishing point, beyond which only "influences" lie. But the writer of the story, bound in the opposite direction, works into the open. The choices multiply, become more complicated and with more hanging on them, as with everything else that has a life and moves. "This story promises me fear and joy and so I write it" has been the writer's beginning. The critic, coming to the end of his trail, may call out the starting point he's found, but the writer knew his starting point first and for what it was—the jumping-off place. And all along, the character of the choices—the critic's decisions and the writer's—is wholly different. I think that the writer's outbound choices were to him the *believable* ones, not necessarily defensible on other grounds; impelled, not subject to scheme but to feeling; that they came with an arrow inside them. They have been *fiction's* choices: one-way and fateful; strict as art, obliged as feeling, powerful in their authenticity.

The story and its analysis are not mirror-opposites of each other. They are not reflections, either one. Criticism indeed is an art, as a story is, but only the story is to some degree a vision; there is no explanation outside fiction for what its writer is learning to do. The simplest-appearing work may have been brought off (when it does not fail) on the sharp edge of experiment, and it was for this its writer was happy to leave behind him all he knew before, and the safety of that, when he began the new story.

•

I feel that our ever-changing outside world and some learn-able lessons about writing fiction are always waiting side by side for us to put into connection, if we can. A writer should say this only of himself and offer an example. In a story I wrote recently called "No Place for You, My Love," the outside world—a defi-nite place in it, of course—not only suggested how to write it but repudiated a way I had already tried. What follows has no claim to be critical analysis; it can be called a piece of hindsight from a working point of view.

What changed my story was a trip. I was invited to drive with an acquaintance, one summer day, down south of New Orleans to see that country for the first (and so far, only) time; and when I got back home, full of the landscape I'd seen, I real-ized that without being aware of it at the time, I had treated the story to my ride, and it had come into my head in an altogether new form. I set to work and wrote the new version from scratch.

As first written, the story told, in subjective terms, of a girl in a claustrophobic predicament: she was caught fast in the over-famil-iar, monotonous life of her small town, and immobilized further by a prolonged and hopeless love affair; she could see no way out. As a result of my ride, I extricated—not the girl, but the story.

This character had been well sealed inside her world, by nature and circumstance, just where I'd put her. But she was sealed in to the detriment of the story, because I'd made hers the point of view. The primary step now was getting outside her mind; on that instant I made her a girl from the Middle West. (She'd been before what I knew best, a Southerner.) I kept out-side her by taking glimpses of her through the eyes of a total stranger: casting off the half-dozen familiars the first girl had around her, I invented a single new character, a man whom I brought into the story *to be* a stranger, and I was to keep out of his mind, too. I had double-locked the doors behind me.

It would have been for nothing had the original impulse behind the story not proved itself alive; it now took on new energy. That country—that once-submerged, strange land of "south from South"—which had so stamped itself upon my imagination put in an unmistakable claim now as the very image of the story's predicament. It pointed out to me at the same time where the real point of view belonged. Once I'd escaped those characters' minds, I saw it was outside them—suspended, hung in the air between two people, fished alive from the surrounding scene. As I wrote further into the story, something more real, more essential, than the characters were on their own was revealing itself. In effect, though the characters numbered only two, there had come to be a sort of third character along on the ride—the presence of a relationship between the two. It was what grew up between them meeting as strangers, went on the excursion with them, nodded back and forth from one to the other—listening, watching, persuading or denying them, enlarging or diminishing them, forgetful sometimes of why they were or what they were doing here—in its domain—and helping or betraying them along.

(Here I think it perhaps should be remembered that characters in a short story have not the size and importance and capacity for development they have in a novel, but are subservient altogether to the story as a whole.)

This third character's role was that of hypnosis—it was what a relationship *can do,* be it however brief, tentative, potential, happy or sinister, ordinary or extraordinary. I wanted to suggest that its being took shape as the strange, compulsive journey itself, was palpable as its climate and mood, the heat of the day—but was its spirit too, a spirit that held territory, that which is seen fleeting past by two vulnerable people who might seize hands on the run. There are moments in the story when I say neither "she felt" nor "he felt" but "they felt."

This is to grant that I rode out of the old story on the back of the girl and then threw away the girl; but I saved my story, for, entirely different as the second version was, it was what I wanted to tell. Now my subject was out in the open, provided at the same time with a place to happen and a way to say it was happening. All I had to do was recognize it, which I did a little late.

Anyone who has visited the actual scene of this story will possibly recognize it when he meets it here, for the story is visual and the place is out of the ordinary. The connection between a story and its setting may not always be so plain. For no matter whether the "likeness" is there for all to see or not, the place, once entered into the writer's mind in a story, is, in the course of writing the story, *functional.*

Thus I wanted to make seen and believed what was to me, in my story's grip, literally apparent—that secret and shadow are taken away in this country by the merciless light that prevails there, by the river that is like an exposed vein of ore, the road that descends as one with the heat—its nerve (these are all terms in the story), and that the heat is also a visual illusion, shimmering and dancing over the waste that stretches ahead. I was writing of a real place, but doing so in order to write about my subject. I was writing of exposure, and the shock of the world; in the end I tried to make the story's inside outside and then leave the shell behind.

The vain courting of imperviousness in the face of exposure is this little story's plot. Deliver us all from the naked in heart, the girls thinks (this is what I kept of her). "So strangeness gently steels us," I read today in a poem of Richard Wilbur's. Riding down together into strange country is danger, a play at danger, secretly poetic, and the characters, in attempting it as a mutual feat, admit nothing to each other except the wicked heat and its comical inconvenience. The only time they will yield or touch is while they are dancing in the crowd that to them is comically unlikely (hence insulating, non-conducting) or taking a kiss out-side time. Nevertheless it happens that they go along aware, from moment to moment, as one: as my third character, the straining, hallucinatory eyes and ears, the roused-up sentient being of that place. Exposure begins in intuition; and the intuition comes to its end in showing the heart that has expected, while it dreads, that exposure. Writing it as I'd done before, as a story of conceal-ment, in terms of the hermetic and the familiar, had somehow resulted in my own effective concealment of what I meant to show.

Now, the place had suggested to me that something demon-aic was called for—the speed of the ride pitted against the dan-ger of an easy or conventionally tempting sympathy, the heat that in itself drives on the driver in the face of an inimical world. Something wilder than ordinary communication between well-disposed strangers, and more ruthless and more tender, more pressing and acute, than their automatic, saving ironies and graces, I felt, and do so often feel, has to come up against a world like that.

I did my best to merge, or even to identify, the abstract with the concrete as it became possible in this story—where setting, characters, mood, and method of writing all worked as parts of the same thing and subject to related laws and conditionings. The story *had* to be self-evident, and to hold its speed to the end—a speed I think of as racing, though it may not seem so to the reader.

Above all, I had no wish to sound mystical, but I admit that I did expect to sound mysterious now and then, if I could: this was a circumstantial, realistic story in which the reality *was* mys-tery. The cry that rose up at the story's end was, I hope unmis-takably, the cry of that doomed relationship—personal, mortal, psychic—admitted in order to be denied, a cry that the charac-ters were first able (and prone) to listen to, and then able in part to ignore. The cry was authentic to my story: the end of a journey *can* set up a cry, the shallowest provocation to sympathy and love does hate to give up the ghost. A relationship of the most fleeting kind has the power inherent to loom like a genie—to become vocative at the last, as it has already become present and taken up room; as it has spread out as a destination however unlikely; as it has glimmered and rushed by in the dark and dust outside, showing occasional points of fire. Relationship *is* a pervading and changing mystery; it is not words that make it so in life, but words have to make it so in a story. Brutal or lovely, the mystery waits for people wherever they go, whatever extreme they run to.

I had got back at the end of the new story to suggesting what I had taken as the point of departure in the old, but there was no question in my mind which story was nearer the mark of my intention. This may not reflect very well on the brightness of the author at work; it may cause a reader to wonder how often a story has to rescue itself. I think it goes to show, all the same, that subject, method, form, style, all wait upon—indeed hang upon—a sort of double thunderclap at the author's ears: the break of the living world upon what is already stirring inside the mind, and the answering impulse that in a moment of high consciousness fuses impact and image and fires them off together. There never really was a sound, but the impact is always recognizable, granting the author's sensitivity and sense; and if the impulse so projected is to some degree fulfilled, it may give some pleasure in its course to the writer and reader. The living world itself remains just the same as it always was, and luckily enough for the story, among other things, for it can test and talk back to the story any day in the week. Between the writer and the story he writes, *there* is the undying third character.

THE IGNORED LESSON
OF ANNE FRANK
1960

In 1939, Austrian-born Bruno Bettelheim emigrated to the
United States. Within a few years of his arrival, he was a respected teacher
at the University of Chicago and a child psychologist of national fame.
His books, *Love Is Not Enough: The Treatment of Emotionally Disturbed
Children* (1950), *The Informed Heart: Autonomy in a Mass Age* (1960),
and *The Uses of Enchantment: The Meaning and Importance of Fairy Tales*
(1976), combined traditional psychoanalysis, developmental psychology,
and social commentary. His essay "The Ignored Lesson of Anne Frank,"
published in 1960 in *Harper's Magazine,* looks beyond his usual themes of
childhood anxiety and the nature of modern America to consider different responses to the Nazi menace in the 1930s and universal attitudes
toward evil. Bettelheim had personal experience of that evil. He spent a
year in the concentration camps at Dachau and Buchenwald before leaving Europe on the eve of the Second World War.

WHEN THE WORLD FIRST LEARNED about the
Nazi concentration and death camps, most civilized
people felt the horrors committed in them to be so
uncanny as to be unbelievable. It came as a severe shock that
supposedly civilized nations could stoop to such inhuman acts.
The implication that modern man has such inadequate control
over his cruel and destructive proclivities was felt as a threat to
our views of ourselves and our humanity. Three different psy-
chological mechanisms were most frequently used for dealing
with the appalling revelation of what had gone on in the
camps:

(1) its applicability to man in general was denied by asserting—contrary to evidence—that the acts of torture and mass murder were committed by a small group of insane or perverted persons;

(2) the truth of the reports was denied by declaring them vastly exaggerated and ascribing them to propaganda (this originated with the German government, which called all reports on terror in the camps "horror propaganda"—*Greuelpropaganda*);

(3) the reports were believed, but the knowledge of the horror repressed as soon as possible.

All three mechanisms could be seen at work after liberation of those prisoners remaining. At first, after the discovery of the camps and their death-dealing, a wave of extreme outrage swept the Allied nations. It was soon followed by a general repression of the discovery in people's minds. Possibly this reaction was due to something more than the blow dealt to modern man's narcissism by the realization that cruelty is still rampant among men. Also present may have been the dim but extremely threatening realization that the modern state now has available the means for changing personality, and for destroying millions it deems undesirable. The ideas that in our day a people's personalities might be changed against their will by the state, and that other populations might be wholly or partially exterminated, are so fearful that one tries to free oneself of them and their impact by defensive denial, or by repression.

The extraordinary world-wide success of the book, play, and movie *The Diary of Anne Frank* suggests the power of the desire to counteract the realization of the personality-destroying and murderous nature of the camps by concentrating all attention on what is experienced as a demonstration that private and intimate life can continue to flourish even under the direct persecution by the most ruthless totalitarian system. And this although Anne Frank's fate demonstrates how efforts at disregarding in private life what goes on around one in society can hasten one's own destruction.

What concerns me here is not what actually happened to the Frank family, how they tried—and failed—to survive their terrible ordeal. It would be very wrong to take apart so humane and moving a story, which aroused so much well-merited compassion for gentle Anne Frank and her tragic fate. What is at issue is the universal and uncritical response to her diary and to the play and movie based on it, and what this reaction tells about our attempts to cope with the feelings her fate—used by us to serve as a symbol of a most human reaction to Nazi terror—arouses in us. I believe that the world-wide acclaim given her story cannot be explained unless we recognize in it our wish to forget the gas chambers, and our effort to do so by glorifying the ability to retreat into an extremely private, gentle, sensitive world, and there to cling as much as possible to what have been one's usual daily attitudes and activities, although surrounded by a maelstrom apt to engulf one at any moment.

The Frank family's attitude that life could be carried on as before may well have been what led to their destruction. By eulogizing how they lived in their hiding place while neglecting to examine first whether it was a reasonable or an effective choice, we were able to ignore the crucial lesson of their story—that such an attitude can be fatal in extreme circumstances.

While the Franks were making their preparations for going passively into hiding, thousands of other Jews in Holland (as elsewhere in Europe) were trying to escape to the free world, in order to survive and/or fight. Others who could not escape went underground—into hiding—each family member with, for example, a different gentile family. We gather from the diary, however, that the chief desire of the Frank family was to continue living as nearly as possible in the same fashion to which they had been accustomed in happier times.

Little Anne, too, wanted only to go on with life as usual, and what else could she have done but fall in with the pattern her parents created for her existence? But hers was not a necessary fate, much less a heroic one; it was a terrible but also a senseless fate. Anne had a good chance to survive, as did many Jewish children in Holland. But she would have had to leave her parents and go to live with a gentile Dutch family, posing as their own child, something her parents would have had to arrange for her.

Everyone who recognized the obvious knew that the hardest way to go underground was to do it as a family; to hide out together made detection by the SS most likely; and when detected, everybody was doomed. By hiding singly, even when one got caught, the others had a chance to survive. The Franks, with their excellent connections among gentile Dutch families, might well have been able to hide out singly, each with a different family. But instead, the main principle of their planning was continuing their beloved family life—an understandable desire, but highly unrealistic in those times. Choosing any other course would have meant not merely giving up living together, but also realizing the full measure of the danger to their lives.

The Franks were unable to accept that going on living as a family as they had done before the Nazi invasion of Holland was no longer a desirable way of life, much as they loved each other; in fact, for them and others like them, it was most dangerous behavior. But even given their wish not to separate, they failed to make appropriate preparations for what was likely to happen.

There is little doubt that the Franks, who were able to provide themselves with so much while arranging for going into hiding, and even while hiding, could have provided themselves with some weapons had they wished. Had they had a gun, Mr. Frank could have shot down at least one or two of the "green police" who came for them. There was no surplus of such police, and the loss of an SS with every Jew arrested would have noticeably hindered the functioning of the police state. Even a butcher knife, which they certainly could have taken with them into hiding, could have been used by them in self-defense. The fate of the Franks wouldn't have been very different, because they all died anyway except for Anne's father. But they could have sold their lives for a high price, instead of walking to their death. Still, although one must assume that Mr. Frank would have fought courageously, as we know he did when a soldier in the first World War, it is not everybody who can plan to kill those who are bent on killing him, although many who would not be ready to contemplate doing so would be willing to kill those who are bent on murdering not only them but also their wives and little daughters.

An entirely different matter would have been planning for escape in case of discovery. The Franks' hiding place had only one entrance; it did not have any other exit. Despite this fact, during their many months of hiding, they did not try to devise one. Nor did they make other plans for escape, such as that one of the family members—as likely as not Mr. Frank—would try to detain the police in the narrow entrance way—maybe even fight them, as suggested above—thus giving other members of the family a chance to escape, either by reaching the roofs of adjacent houses, or down a ladder into the alley behind the house in which they were living.

Any of this would have required recognizing and accepting the desperate straits in which they found themselves, and concentrating on how best to cope with them. This was quite possible to do, even under the terrible conditions in which the Jews found themselves after the Nazi occupation of Holland. It can be seen from many other accounts, for example from the story of Marga Minco, a girl of about Anne Frank's age who lived to tell about it. Her parents had planned that when the police should come for them, the father would try to detain them by arguing and fighting with them, to give the wife and daughter a chance to escape through a rear door. Unfortunately it did not quite work out this way, and both parents got killed. But their short-lived resistance permitted their daughter to make her escape as planned and to reach a Dutch family who saved her.[1]

This is not mentioned as a criticism that the Frank family did not plan or behave along similar lines. A family has every right to arrange their life as they wish or think best, and to take the risks they want to take. My point is not to criticize what the Franks did, but only the universal admiration of their way of coping, or rather of not coping. The story of little Marga who survived, every bit as touching, remains totally neglected by comparison.

Many Jews—unlike the Franks, who through listening to British radio news were better informed than most—had no detailed knowledge of the extermination camps. Thus it was easier for them to make themselves believe that complete compliance with even the most outrageously debilitating and degrading Nazi orders might offer a chance for survival. But neither tremendous anxiety that inhibits clear thinking and with it well-planned and determined action, nor ignorance about what happened to those who responded with passive waiting for being rounded up for their extermination, can explain the reaction of audiences to the play and movie retelling Anne's story, which are all about such waiting that results finally in destruction.

I think it is the fictitious ending that explains the enormous success of this play and movie. At the conclusion we hear Anne's voice from the beyond, saying, "In spite of everything, I still believe that people are really good at heart." This improbable sentiment is supposedly from a girl who had been starved to death, had watched her sister meet the same fate before she did, knew that her mother had been murdered, and had watched untold thousands of adults and children being killed. This statement is not justified by anything Anne actually told her diary.

Going on with intimate family living, no matter how dangerous it might be to survival, was fatal to all too many during the Nazi regime. And if all men are good, then indeed we can all go on with living our lives as we have been accustomed to in times of undisturbed safety and can afford to forget about Auschwitz. But Anne, her sister, her mother, may well have died because her parents could not get themselves to believe in Auschwitz.

While play and movie are ostensibly about Nazi persecution and destruction, in actuality what we watch is the way that, despite this terror, lovable people manage to continue living their satisfying intimate lives with each other. The heroine grows from a child into a young adult as normally as any other girl would, despite the most abnormal conditions of all other aspects of her existence, and that of her family. Thus the play reassures us that despite the destructiveness of Nazi racism and tyranny in general, it is possible to disregard it in one's private life much of the time, even if one is Jewish.

True, the ending happens just as the Franks and their friends had feared all along: their hiding place is discovered, and they are carried away to their doom. But the fictitious declaration of faith in the goodness of all men which concludes the play falsely reassures us since it impresses on us that in the combat between Nazi terror and continuance of intimate family living the latter wins out, since Anne has the last word. This is simply contrary to fact, because it was she who got killed. Her seeming survival through her moving statement about the goodness of men releases us effectively of the need to cope with the problems Auschwitz presents. That is why we are so relieved by her statement. It explains why millions loved play and movie, because while it confronts us with the fact that Auschwitz existed, it encourages us at the same time to ignore any of its implications. If all men are good at heart, there never really was an Auschwitz; nor is there any possibility that it may recur.

The desire of Anne Frank's parents not to interrupt their intimate family living, and their inability to plan more effectively for their survival, reflect the failure of all too many others faced with the threat of Nazi terror. It is a failure that deserves close examination because of the inherent warnings it contains for us, the living.

Submission to the threatening power of the Nazi state often led both to the disintegration of what had once seemed well-integrated personalities and to a return to an immature disregard for the dangers of reality. Those Jews who submitted passively to Nazi persecution came to depend on primitive and infantile thought processes: wishful thinking and disregard for the possibility of death. Many persuaded themselves that they, out of all the others, would be spared. Many more simply disbelieved in the possibility of their own death. Not believing in it, they did not take what seemed to them desperate precautions, such as giving up everything to hide out singly; or trying to escape even if it meant risking their lives in doing so; or preparing to fight for their lives when no escape was possible and death had become an immediate possibility. It is true that defending their lives in active combat before they were rounded up to be transported into the camps might have hastened their deaths, and so, up to a point, they were protecting themselves by "rolling with the punches" of the enemy.

But the longer one rolls with the punches dealt not by the normal vagaries of life, but by one's eventual executioner, the more likely it becomes that one will no longer have the strength to resist when death becomes imminent. This is particularly true if yielding to the enemy is accompanied not by a commensurate strengthening of the personality, but by an inner disintegration. We can observe such a process among the Franks, who bickered with each other over trifles, instead of supporting each other's ability to resist the demoralizing impact of their living conditions.

Those who faced up to the announced intentions of the Nazis prepared for the worst as a real and imminent possibility. It meant risking one's life for a self-chosen purpose, but in doing so, creating at least a small chance for saving one's own life or those of others, or both. When Jews in Germany were restricted to their homes, those who did not succumb to inertia took the new restrictions as a warning that it was high time to go underground, join the resistance movement, provide themselves with forged papers, and so on, if they had not done so long ago. Many of them survived.

Some distant relatives of mine may furnish an example. Early in the war, a young man living in a small Hungarian town banded together with a number of other Jews to prepare against a German invasion. As soon as the Nazis imposed curfews on the Jews, his group left for Budapest—because the bigger capital city with its greater anonymity offered chances for escaping detection. Similar groups from other towns converged in Budapest and joined forces. From among themselves they selected typically "Aryan" looking men who equipped themselves with false papers and immediately joined the Hungarian SS. These spies were then able to warn of impending persecution and raids.

Many of these groups survived intact. Furthermore, they had also equipped themselves with small arms, so that if they were detected, they could put up enough of a fight for the majority to escape while a few would die fighting to make the escape possible. A few of the Jews who had joined the SS were discovered and immediately shot, probably a death preferable to one in the gas chambers. But most of even these Jews survived, hiding within the SS until liberation.

Compare these arrangements not just to the Franks' selection of a hiding place that was basically a trap without an outlet but with Mr. Frank's teaching typically academic high-school subjects to his children rather than how to make a getaway: a token of his inability to face the seriousness of the threat of death. Teaching high-school subjects had, of course, its constructive aspects. It relieved the ever-present anxiety about their fate to some degree by concentrating on different matters, and by implication it encouraged hope for a future in which such knowledge would be useful. In this sense such teaching was purposeful, but it was erroneous in that it took the place of much more pertinent teaching and planning: how best to try to escape when detected.

Unfortunately the Franks were by no means the only ones who, out of anxiety, became unable to contemplate their true situation and with it to plan accordingly. Anxiety, and the wish to counteract it by clinging to each other, and to reduce its sting by continuing as much as possible with their usual way of life incapacitated many, particularly when survival plans required changing radically old ways of living that they cherished, and which had become their only source of satisfaction.

My young relative, for example, was unable to persuade other members of his family to go with him when he left the small town where he had lived with them. Three times, at tremendous risk to himself, he returned to plead with his relatives, pointing out first the growing persecution of the Jews, and later the fact that transport to the gas chambers had already begun. He could not convince these Jews to leave their homes and break up their families to go singly into hiding.

As their desperation mounted, they clung more determined-ly to their old living arrangements and to each other, became less able to consider giving up the possessions they had accumu-lated through hard work over a lifetime. The more severely their freedom to act was reduced, and what little they were still per-mitted to do restricted by insensible and degrading regulations imposed by the Nazis, the more did they become unable to con-template independent action. Their life energies drained out of them, sapped by their ever-greater anxiety. The less they found strength in themselves, the more they held on to the little that was left of what had given them security in the past—their old surroundings, their customary way of life, their possessions—all these seemed to give their lives some permanency, offer some symbols of security. Only what had once been symbols of securi-ty now endangered life, since they were excuses for avoiding change. On each successive visit the young man found his rela-tives more incapacitated, less willing or able to take his advice, more frozen into inactivity, and with it further along the way to the crematoria where, in fact, they all died.

Levin renders a detailed account of the desperate but fruit-less efforts made by small Jewish groups determined to survive to try to save the rest. She tells how messengers were "sent into the provinces to warn Jews that deportation meant death, but their warnings were ignored because most Jews refused to con-template their own annihilation."[2] I believe the reason for such refusal has to be found in their inability to take action. If we are certain that we are helpless to protect ourselves against the danger of destruction, we cannot contemplate it. We can con-sider the danger only as long as we believe there are ways to protect ourselves, to fight back, to escape. If we are convinced none of this is possible for us, then there is no point in think-ing about the danger; on the contrary, it is best to refuse to do so.

As a prisoner in Buchenwald, I talked to hundreds of German Jewish prisoners who were brought there as part of the huge pogrom in the wake of the murder of vom Rath in the fall of 1938. I asked them why they had not left Germany, given the utterly degrading conditions they had been subjected to. Their answer was: How could we leave? It would have meant giving up our homes, our work, our sources of income. Having been deprived by Nazi persecution and degradation of much of their self-respect, they had become unable to give up what still gave them a semblance of it: their earthly belongings. But instead of using possessions, they became captivated by them, and this possession by earthly goods became the fatal mask for their possession by anxiety, fear, and denial.

How the investment of personal property with one's life energy could make people die bit by bit was illustrated throughout the Nazi persecution of the Jews. At the time of the first boycott of Jewish stores, the chief external goal of the Nazis was to acquire the possessions of the Jews. They even let Jews take some things out of the country at that time if they would leave the bulk of their property behind. For a long time the intention of the Nazis, and the goal of their first discriminatory laws, was to force undesirable minorities, including Jews, into emigration.

Although the extermination policy was in line with the inner logic of Nazi racial ideology, one may wonder whether the idea that millions of Jews (and other foreign nationals) could be submitted to extermination did not partially result from seeing the degree of degradation Jews accepted without fighting back. When no violent resistance occurred, persecution of the Jews worsened, slow step by slow step.

Many Jews who on the invasion of Poland were able to survey their situation and draw the right conclusions survived the Second World War. As the Germans approached, they left everything behind and fled to Russia, much as they distrusted and disliked the Soviet system. But there, while badly treated, they could at least survive. Those who stayed on in Poland believing they could go on with life-as-before sealed their fate. Thus in the deepest sense the walk to the gas chamber was only the last consequence of these Jews' inability to comprehend what was in store; it was the final step of surrender to the death instinct, which might also be called the principle of inertia. The first step was taken long before arrival at the death camp.

We can find a dramatic demonstration of how far the surrender to inertia can be carried, and the wish not to know because knowing would create unbearable anxiety, in an experience of Olga Lengyel.[3] She reports that although she and her fellow prisoners lived just a few hundred yards from the crematoria and the gas chambers and knew what they were for, most prisoners denied knowledge of them for months. If they had grasped their true situation, it might have helped them save either the lives they themselves were fated to lose, or the lives of others.

When Mrs. Lengyel's fellow prisoners were selected to be sent to the gas chambers, they did not try to break away from the group, as she successfully did. Worse, the first time she tried to escape the gas chambers, some of the other selected prisoners told the supervisors that she was trying to get away. Mrs. Lengyel desperately asks the question: How was it possible that people denied the existence of the gas chambers when all day long they saw the crematoria burning and smelled the odor of burning flesh? Why did they prefer ignoring the exterminations to fighting for their very own lives? She can offer no explanation, only the observation that they resented anyone who tried to save himself from the common fate, because they lacked enough courage to risk action themselves. I believe they did it because they had given up their will to live and permitted their death tendencies to engulf them. As a result, such prisoners were in the thrall of the murdering SS not only physically but also psychologically, while this was not true for those prisoners who still had a grip on life.

Some prisoners even began to serve their executioners, to help speed the death of their own kind. Then things had progressed beyond simple inertia to the death instinct running rampant. Those who tried to serve their executioners in what were once their civilian capacities were merely continuing life as usual and thereby opening the door to their death.

For example, Mrs. Lengyel speaks of Dr. Mengele, SS physician at Auschwitz, as a typical example of the "business as usual" attitude that enabled some prisoners, and certainly the SS, to retain whatever balance they could despite what they were doing. She describes how Dr. Mengele took all correct medical precautions during childbirth, rigorously observing all aseptic principles, cutting the umbilical cord with greatest care, etc. But only half an hour later he sent mother and infant to be burned in the crematorium.

Having made his choice, Dr. Mengele and others like him had to delude themselves to be able to live with themselves and their experience. Only one personal document on the subject has come to my attention, that of Dr. Nyiszli, a prisoner serving as "research physician" at Auschwitz.[4] How Dr. Nyiszli deluded himself can be seen, for example, in the way he repeatedly refers to himself as working in Auschwitz as a physician, although he worked as the assistant of a criminal murderer. He speaks of the Institute for Race, Biological, and Anthropological Investigation as "one of the most qualified medical centers of the Third Reich," although it was devoted to proving falsehoods. That Nyiszli was a doctor didn't alter the fact that he—like any of the prisoner foremen who served the SS better than some SS were willing to serve it—was a participant in the crimes of the SS. How could he do it and live with himself?

The answer is: by taking pride in his professional skills, irrespective of the purpose they served. Dr. Nyiszli and Dr. Mengele were only two among hundreds of other—and far more prominent—physicians who participated in the Nazis' murderous pseudo-scientific human experiments. It was the peculiar pride of these men in their professional skill and knowledge, without regard for moral implications, that made them so dangerous. Although the concentration camps and crematoria are no longer here, this kind of pride still remains with us; it is characteristic of a modern society in which fascination with technical competence has dulled concern for human feelings. Auschwitz is gone, but so long as this attitude persists, we shall not be safe from cruel indifference to life at the core.

I have met many Jews as well as gentile anti-Nazis, similar to the activist group in Hungary described earlier, who survived in Nazi Germany and in the occupied countries. These people realized that when a world goes to pieces and inhumanity reigns supreme, man cannot go on living his private life as he was wont to do, and would like to do; he cannot, as the loving head of a family, keep the family living together peacefully, undisturbed by the surrounding world; nor can he continue to take pride in his profession or possessions, when either will deprive him of his humanity, if not also of his life. In such times, one must radically reevaluate all of what one has done, believed in, and stood for in order to know how to act. In short, one has to take a stand on the new reality—a firm stand, not one of retirement into an even more private world.

If today, Negroes in Africa march against the guns of a police that defends *apartheid*—even if hundreds of dissenters are shot down and tens of thousands rounded up in camps—their fight will sooner or later assure them of a chance for liberty and equality. Millions of the Jews of Europe who did not or could not escape in time or go underground as many thousands did, could at least have died fighting as some did in the Warsaw ghetto at the end, instead of passively waiting to be rounded up for their own extermination.

---

[1] Marga Minco, *Bitter Herbs* (New York: Oxford University Press, 1960).

[2] Nora Levin, *The Holocaust* (New York: Thomas Y. Crowell, 1968).

[3] Olga Lengyel, *Five Chimneys: The Story of Auschwitz* (Chicago: Ziff-Davis, 1947).

[4] Miklos Nyiszli, *Auschwitz: A Doctor's Eyewitness Account* (New York: Frederick Fell, 1960).

Martin Luther King, Jr.

LETTER FROM
A BIRMINGHAM JAIL
1963

"Letter from a Birmingham Jail" was written in longhand on scraps of paper smuggled into the jail cell where Martin Luther King, Jr., was imprisoned in 1963. He had been arrested for his participation in nonviolent demonstrations against segregation in that city. Eight white religious leaders, including the Episcopal bishop of Alabama, spoke out against the demonstrations, urging patience and suggesting that dramatic protests were likely to do more harm than good.

In the guise of a letter responding to the ministers, this unusual document presents the reader with an overview of the civil rights movement, an intellectual history of civil disobedience, and (not least) a stirring example of the rhetoric of anger and moral challenge.

WHILE CONFINED HERE in the Birmingham city jail, I came across your recent statement calling our present activities "unwise and untimely." Seldom, if ever, do I pause to answer criticism of my work and ideas. If I sought to answer all of the criticisms that cross my desk, my secretaries would be engaged in little else in the course of the day, and I would have no time for constructive work. But since I feel that you are men of genuine good will and your criticisms are sincerely set forth, I would like to answer your statement in what I hope will be patient and reasonable terms.

I think I should give the reason for my being in Birmingham, since you have been influenced by the argument of "outsiders coming in." I have the honor of serving as president of the Southern Christian Leadership Conference, an organization operating in every Southern state, with headquarters in Atlanta, Georgia. We have some eighty-five affiliate organizations all across the South, one being the Alabama Christian Movement for Human Rights. Whenever necessary and possible, we share staff, educational and financial resources with our affiliates. Several months ago our local affiliate here in Birmingham invited us to be on call to engage in a nonviolent direct-action program if such were deemed necessary. We readily consented, and when the hour came we lived up to our promises. So I am here, along with several members of my staff, because we were invited here. I am here because I have basic organizational ties here.

Beyond this, I am in Birmingham because injustice is here. Just as the eighth-century prophets left their little villages and carried their "thus saith the Lord" far beyond the boundaries of their hometowns; and just as the Apostle Paul left his little village of Tarsus and carried the gospel of Jesus Christ to practically every hamlet and city of the Greco-Roman world, I too am compelled to carry the gospel of freedom beyond my particular hometown. Like Paul, I must constantly respond to the Macedonian call for aid.

Moreover, I am cognizant of the interrelatedness of all communities and states. I cannot sit idly by in Atlanta and not be concerned about what happens in Birmingham. Injustice anywhere is a threat to justice everywhere. We are caught in an inescapable network of mutuality, tied in a single garment of destiny. Whatever affects one directly affects all indirectly. Never again can we afford to live with the narrow, provincial "outside agitator" idea. Anyone who lives inside the United States can never be considered an outsider.

You deplore the demonstrations that are presently taking place in Birmingham. But I am sorry that your statement did not express a similar concern for the conditions that brought the demonstrations into being. I am sure that each of you would want to go beyond the superficial social analyst who looks merely at effects and does not grapple with underlying causes. I would not hesitate to say that it is unfortunate that so-called demonstrations are taking place in Birmingham at this time, but I would say in more emphatic terms that it is even more unfortunate that the white power structure of this city left the Negro community with no other alternative.

In any nonviolent campaign there are four basic steps: collection of the facts to determine whether injustices are alive, negotiation, self-purification, and direct action. We have gone through all of these steps in Birmingham. There can be no gainsaying of the fact that racial injustice engulfs this community. Birming-ham is probably the most thoroughly segregated city in the United States. Its ugly record of police brutality is known in every section of this country. Its unjust treatment of Negroes in the courts is a notorious reality. There have been more unsolved bombings of Negro homes and churches in Birmingham than in any other city in this nation. These are the hard, brutal, and unbelievable facts. On the basis of them, Negro leaders sought to negotiate with the city fathers. But the political leaders consistently refused to engage in good-faith negotiation.

Then came the opportunity last September to talk with some of the leaders of the economic community. In these negotiating sessions certain promises were made by the merchants, such as the promise to remove the humiliating racial signs from the stores. On the basis of these promises, Reverend Shuttlesworth and the leaders of the Alabama Christian Movement for Human Rights agreed to call a moratorium on any type of demonstration. As the weeks and months unfolded, we realized that we were the victims of a broken promise. The signs remained. As in so many experiences of the past, we were confronted with blasted hopes, and the dark shadow of a deep disappointment settled upon us. So we had no alternative except that of preparing for direct action, whereby we would present our very bodies as a means of laying our case before the conscience of the local and national community. We were not unmindful of the difficulties involved. So we decided to go through a process of self-purification. We started having workshops on nonviolence and repeatedly asked ourselves the questions, "Are you able to accept blows without retaliating?" and "Are you able to endure the ordeals of jail?" We decided to set our direct-action program around the Easter season, realizing that, with exception of Christmas, this was the largest shopping period of the year. Knowing that a strong economic withdrawal program would be the by-product of direct action, we felt that this was the best time to bring pressure on the merchants for the needed changes. Then it occurred to us that the March election was ahead, and so we speedily decided to postpone action until after election day. When we discovered that Mr. Conner was in the runoff, we decided again to postpone action so that the demonstration could not be used to cloud the issues. At this time we agreed to begin our nonviolent witness the day after the runoff.

This reveals that we did not move irresponsibly into direct action. We, too, wanted to see Mr. Conner defeated, so we went through postponement after postponement to aid in this community need. After this we felt that direct action could be delayed no longer.

You may well ask, "Why direct action, why sit-ins, marches, and so forth? Isn't negotiation a better path?" You are exactly right in your call for negotiation. Indeed, this is the purpose of direct action. Nonviolent direct action seeks to create such a crisis and establish such creative tension that a community that has consistently refused to negotiate is forced to confront the issue.

It seeks so to dramatize the issue that it can no longer be ignored. I just referred to the creation of tension as a part of the work of the nonviolent resister. This may sound rather shocking. But I must confess that I am not afraid of the word "tension." I have earnestly worked and preached against violent tension, but there is a type of constructive nonviolent tension that is necessary for growth. Just as Socrates felt that it was necessary to create a tension in the mind so that individuals could rise from the bondage of myths and half-truths to the unfettered realm of creative analysis and objective appraisal, we must see the need of having nonviolent gadflies to create the kind of tension in society that will help men to rise from the dark depths of prejudice and racism to the majestic heights of understanding and brotherhood. So, the purpose of direct action is to create a situation so crisis-packed that it will inevitably open the door to negotiation. We therefore concur with you in your call for negotiation. Too long has our beloved Southland been bogged down in the tragic attempt to live in monologue rather than dialogue.

One of the basic points in your statement is that our acts are untimely. Some have asked, "Why didn't you give the new administration time to act?" The only answer that I can give to this inquiry is that the new administration must be prodded about as much as the outgoing one before it acts. We will be sadly mistaken if we feel that the election of Mr. Boutwell will bring the millennium to Birmingham. While Mr. Boutwell is much more articulate and gentle than Mr. Conner, they are both segregationists, dedicated to the task of maintaining the status quo. The hope I see in Mr. Boutwell is that he will be reasonable enough to see the futility of massive resistance to desegregation. But he will not see this without pressure from the devotees of civil rights. My friends, I must say to you that we have not made a single gain in civil rights without determined legal and nonviolent pressure. History is the long and tragic story of the fact that privileged groups seldom give up their privileges voluntarily. Individuals may see the moral light and voluntarily give up their unjust posture; but, as Reinhold Niebuhr has reminded us, groups are more immoral than individuals.

We know through painful experience that freedom is never voluntarily given by the oppressor; it must be demanded by the oppressed. Frankly, I have never yet engaged in a direct-action movement that was "well timed" according to the timetable of those who have not suffered unduly from the disease of segregation. For years now I have heard the word "wait." It rings in the ear of every Negro with a piercing familiarity. This "wait" has almost always meant "never." It has been a tranquilizing thalidomide, relieving the emotional stress for a moment, only to give birth to an ill-formed infant of frustration. We must come to see with the distinguished jurist of yesterday that "justice too long delayed is justice denied." We have waited for more than three hundred and forty years for our God-given and constitutional rights. The nations of Asia and Africa are moving with jetlike speed toward the goal of political independence, and we still creep at horse-and-buggy pace toward the gaining of a cup of coffee at a lunch counter. I guess it is easy for those who have never felt the stinging darts of segregation to say "wait." But when you have seen vicious mobs lynch your mothers and fathers at will and drown your sisters and brothers at whim; when you have seen hate-filled policemen curse, kick, brutalize, and even kill your black brothers and sisters with impunity; when you see the vast majority of your twenty million Negro brothers smothering in an airtight cage of poverty in the midst of an affluent society; when you suddenly find your tongue twisted and your speech stammering as you seek to explain to your six-year-old daughter why she cannot go to the public amusement park that has just been advertised on television, and see tears welling up in her little eyes when she is told that

Funtown is closed to colored children, and see the depressing clouds of inferiority begin to form in her little mental sky, and see her begin to distort her little personality by unconsciously developing a bitterness toward white people; when you have to concoct an answer for a five-year-old son asking in agonizing pathos, "Daddy, why do white people treat colored people so mean?"; when you take a cross-country drive and find it necessary to sleep night after night in the uncomfortable corners of your automobile because no motel will accept you; when you are humiliated day in and day out by nagging signs reading "white" and "colored"; when your first name becomes "nigger" and your middle name becomes "boy" (however old you are) and your last name becomes "John," and when your wife and mother are never given the respected title "Mrs."; when you are harried by day and haunted by night by the fact that you are a Negro, living constantly at tiptoe stance, never quite knowing what to expect next, and plagued with inner fears and outer resentments; when you are forever fighting a degenerating sense of "nobodyness"—then you will understand why we find it difficult to wait. There comes a time when the cup of endurance runs over and men are no longer willing to be plunged into an abyss of injustice where they experience the bleakness of corroding despair. I hope, sirs, you can understand our legitimate and unavoidable impatience.

You express a great deal of anxiety over our willingness to break laws. This is certainly a legitimate concern. Since we so diligently urge people to obey the Supreme Court's decision of 1954 outlawing segregation in the public schools, it is rather strange and paradoxical to find us consciously breaking laws. One may well ask, "How can you advocate breaking some laws and obeying others?" The answer is found in the fact that there are two types of laws: there are just laws, and there are unjust laws. I would agree with St. Augustine that "An unjust law is no law at all."

Now, what is the difference between the two? How does one determine when a law is just or unjust? A just law is a man-made code that squares with the moral law, or the law of God. An unjust law is a code that is out of harmony with the moral law. To put it in the terms of St. Thomas Aquinas, an unjust law is a human law that is not rooted in eternal and natural law. Any law that uplifts human personality is just. Any law that degrades human personality is unjust. All segregation statues are unjust because segregation distorts the soul and damages the personality. It gives the segregator a false sense of superiority and the segregated a false sense of inferiority. To use the words of Martin Buber, the great Jewish philosopher, segregation substitutes an "I–it" relationship for the "I–thou" relationship and ends up relegating persons to the status of things. So segregation is not only politically, economically, and sociologically unsound, but it is morally wrong and sinful. Paul Tillich has said that sin is separation. Isn't segregation an existential expression of man's tragic separation, an expression of his awful estrangement, his terrible sinfulness? So I can urge men to obey the 1954 decision of the Supreme Court because it is morally right, and I can urge them to disobey segregation ordinances because they are morally wrong.

Let us turn to a more concrete example of just and unjust laws. An unjust law is a code that a majority inflicts on a minority that is not binding on itself. This is difference made legal. On the other hand, a just law is a code that a majority compels a minority to follow, and that it is willing to follow itself. This is sameness made legal.

Let me give another explanation. An unjust law is a code inflicted upon a minority which that minority had no part in enacting or creating because it did not have the unhampered right to vote. Who can say that the legislature of Alabama which set up the segregation laws was democratically elected? Throughout the state of Alabama all types of conniving methods are used to prevent Negroes from becoming registered voters, and there are some counties without a single Negro registered to vote, despite the fact that the Negroes constitute a majority of the population. Can any law set up in such a state be considered democratically structured?

These are just a few examples of unjust and just laws. There are some instances when a law is just on its face and unjust in its application. For instance, I was arrested Friday on a charge of parading without a permit. Now, there is nothing wrong with an ordinance which requires a permit for a parade, but when the ordinance is used to preserve segregation and to deny citizens the First Amendment privilege of peaceful assembly and peaceful protest, then it becomes unjust.

Of course, there is nothing new about this kind of civil disobedience. It was seen sublimely in the refusal of Shadrach, Meshach, and Abednego to obey the laws of Nebuchadnezzar because a higher moral law was involved. It was practiced superbly by the early Christians, who were willing to face hungry lions and the excruciating pain of chopping blocks before submitting to certain unjust laws of the Roman Empire. To a degree, academic freedom is a reality today because Socrates practiced civil disobedience.

We can never forget that everything Hitler did in Germany was "legal" and everything the Hungarian freedom fighters did in Hungary was "illegal." It was "illegal" to aid and comfort a Jew in Hitler's Germany. But I am sure that if I had lived in Germany during that time, I would have aided and comforted my Jewish brothers even though it was illegal. If I lived in a Communist country today where certain principles dear to the Christian faith are suppressed, I believe I would openly advocate disobeying these anti-religious laws.

•

I must make two honest confessions to you, my Christian and Jewish brothers. First, I must confess that over the last few years I have been gravely disappointed with the white moderate. I have almost reached the regrettable conclusion that the Negro's great stumbling block in the stride toward freedom is not the White Citizens Councillor or the Ku Klux Klanner but the white moderate who is more devoted to order than to justice; who prefers a negative peace which is the absence of tension to a positive peace which is the presence of justice; who constantly says, "I agree with you in the goal you seek, but I can't agree with your methods of direct action"; who paternalistically feels that he can set the timetable for another man's freedom; who lives by the myth of time; and who constantly advises the Negro to wait until a "more convenient season." Shallow understanding from people of good will is more frustrating than absolute misunderstanding from people of ill will. Lukewarm acceptance is much more bewildering than outright rejection.

In your statement you asserted that our actions, even though peaceful, must be condemned because they precipitate violence. But can this assertion be logically made? Isn't this like condemning the robbed man because his possession of money precipitated the evil act of robbery? Isn't this like condemning Socrates because his unswerving commitment to truth and his philosophical delvings precipitated the misguided popular mind to make him drink the hemlock? Isn't this like condemning Jesus because His unique God-consciousness and never-ceasing devotion to His will precipitated the evil act of crucifixion? We must come to see, as federal courts have consistently affirmed, that it is immoral to urge an individual to withdraw his efforts to gain his basic constitutional rights because the quest precipitates violence. Society must protect the robbed and punish the robber.

I had also hoped that the white moderate would reject the myth of time. I received a letter this morning from a white brother in Texas which said, "All Christians know that the colored people will receive equal rights eventually, but is it possible that you are in too great of a religious hurry? It has taken Christianity almost 2000 years to accomplish what it has. The teachings of Christ take time to come to earth." All that is said here grows out of a tragic misconception of time. It is the strangely irrational notion that there is something in the very flow of time that will inevitably cure all ills. Actually, time is neutral. It can be used either destructively or constructively. I am coming to feel that the people of ill will have used time much more effectively than the people of good will. We will have to repent in this generation not merely for the vitriolic words and actions of the bad people but for the appalling silence of the good people. We must come to see that human progress never rolls in on wheels of inevitability. It comes through the tireless efforts and persistent work of men willing to be coworkers with God, and without this hard work time itself becomes an ally of the forces of social stagnation.

You spoke of our activity in Birmingham as extreme. At first I was rather disappointed that fellow clergymen would see my nonviolent efforts as those of an extremist. I started thinking about the fact that I stand in the middle of two opposing forces in the Negro community. One is a force of complacency made up of Negroes who, as a result of long years of oppression, have been so completely drained of self-respect and a sense of "somebodyness" that they have adjusted to segregation, and, on the other hand, of a few Negroes in the middle class who, because of a degree of academic and economic security and because at points they profit by segregation, have unconsciously become insensitive to the problems of the masses. The other force is one of bitterness and hatred and comes perilously close to advocating violence. It is expressed in the various black nationalist groups that are springing up over the nation, the largest and best known being Elijah Muhammad's Muslim movement. This movement is nourished by the contemporary frustration over the continued existence of racial discrimination. It is made up of people who have lost faith in America, who have absolutely repudiated Christianity, and who have concluded that the white man is an incurable devil. I have tried to stand between these two forces, saying that we need not follow the do-nothingism of the complacent or the hatred and despair of the black nationalist. There is a more excellent way, of love and nonviolent protest. I'm grateful to God that, through the Negro church, the dimension of nonviolence entered our struggle. If this philosophy had not emerged, I am convinced that by now many streets of the South would be flowing with floods of blood. And I am further convinced that if our white brothers dismiss as "rabble-rousers" and "outside agitators" those of us who are working through the channels of nonviolent direct action and refuse to support our nonviolent efforts, millions of Negroes, out of frustration and despair, will seek solace and security in black nationalist ideologies, a development that will lead inevitably to a frightening racial nightmare.

Oppressed people cannot remain oppressed forever. The urge for freedom will eventually come. This is what has happened to the American Negro. Something within has reminded him of his birthright of freedom; something without has reminded him that he can gain it. Consciously and unconsciously, he has been swept in by what the Germans call the *Zeitgeist,* and with his black brothers of Africa and his brown and yellow brothers of Asia, South America, and the Caribbean, he is moving with a sense of cosmic urgency toward the promised land of racial justice. Recognizing this vital urge that has engulfed the Negro community, one should readily understand public demonstrations. The Negro has many pent-up resentments and latent frustrations. He has to get them out. So let him march sometime; let him have his prayer pilgrimages to the city hall; understand why he must have sit-ins and freedom rides. If his repressed emotions do not come out in these nonviolent ways, they will come out in ominous expressions of violence. This is not a threat; it is a fact of history. So I have not said to my people, "Get rid of your discontent." But I have tried to say that this normal and healthy discontent can be channeled through the creative outlet of nonviolent direct action. Now this approach is being dismissed as extremist. I must admit that I was initially disappointed in being so categorized.

But as I continued to think about the matter, I gradually gained a bit of satisfaction from being considered an extremist. Was not Jesus an extremist in love?—"Love your enemies, bless them that curse you, pray for them that despitefully use you." Was not Amos an extremist for justice?—"Let justice roll down like waters and righteousness like a mighty steam." Was not Paul an extremist for the gospel of Jesus Christ?—"I bear in my body the marks of the Lord Jesus." Was not Martin Luther an extremist?—"Here I stand; I can do no other so help me God." Was not John Bunyan an extremist?—"I will stay in jail to the end of my days before I make a mockery of my conscience." Was not Abraham Lincoln an extremist?—"This nation cannot survive half slave and half free." Was not Thomas Jefferson an extremist?—"We hold these truths to be self-evident, that all men are created equal." So the question is not whether we will be extremist, but what kind of extremists we will be. Will we be extremists for hate, or will we be extremists for love? Will we be extremists for the preservation of injustice, or will we be extremists for the cause of justice?

I had hoped that the white moderate would see this. Maybe

I was too optimistic. Maybe I expected too much. I guess I should have realized that few members of a race that has oppressed another race can understand or appreciate the deep groans and passionate yearnings of those that have been oppressed, and still fewer have the vision to see that injustice must be rooted out by strong, persistent, and determined action. I am thankful, however, that some of our white brothers have grasped the meaning of this social revolution and committed themselves to it. They are still all too small in quantity, but they are big in quality. Some, like Ralph McGill, Lillian Smith, Harry Golden, and James Dabbs, have written about our struggle in eloquent, prophetic, and understanding terms. Others have marched with us down nameless streets of the South. They sat in with us at lunch counters and rode in with us on the freedom rides. They have languished in filthy roach-infested jails, suffering the abuse and brutality of angry policemen who see them as "dirty nigger lovers." They, unlike many of their moderate brothers, have recognized the urgency of the moment and sensed the need for powerful "action" antidotes to combat the disease of segregation.

Let me rush on to mention my other disappointment. I have been disappointed with the white church and its leadership. Of course, there are some notable exceptions. I am not unmindful of the fact that each of you has taken some significant stands on this issue. I commend you, Reverend Stallings, for your Christian stand this past Sunday in welcoming Negroes to your Baptist Church worship service on a nonsegregated basis. I commend the Catholic leaders of this state for integrating Springhill College several years ago.

But despite these notable exceptions, I must honestly reiterate that I have been disappointed with the church. I do not say that as one of those negative critics who can always find something wrong with the church. I say it as a minister of the gospel who loves the church, who was nurtured in its bosom, who has been sustained by its spiritual blessings, and who will remain true to it as long as the cord of life shall lengthen.

I had the strange feeling when I was suddenly catapulted into the leadership of the bus protest in Montgomery several years ago that we would have the support of the white church. I felt that the white ministers, priests, and rabbis of the South would be some of our strongest allies. Instead, some few have been outright opponents, refusing to understand the freedom movement and misrepresenting its leaders; all too many others have been more cautious than courageous and have remained silent behind the anesthetizing security of stained-glass windows.

In spite of my shattered dreams of the past, I came to Birmingham with the hope that the white religious leadership of this community would see the justice of our cause and with deep moral concern serve as the channel through which our just grievances could get to the power structure. I had hoped that each of you would understand. But again I have been disappointed.

I have heard numerous religious leaders of the South call upon their worshipers to comply with a desegregation decision because it is the law, but I have longed to hear white ministers say, follow this decree because integration is morally right and the Negro is your brother. In the midst of blatant injustices inflicted upon the Negro, I have watched white churches stand on the sidelines and merely mouth pious irrelevancies and sanctimonious trivialities. In the midst of a mighty struggle to rid our nation of racial and economic injustice, I have heard so many ministers say, "Those are social issues which the gospel has nothing to do with," and I have watched so many churches commit themselves to a completely other-worldly religion which made a strange distinction between bodies and souls, the sacred and the secular.

There was a time when the church was very powerful. It was during that period that the early Christians rejoiced when they were deemed worthy to suffer for what they believed. In those days the church was not merely a thermometer that recorded the ideas and principles of popular opinion; it was the thermostat that transformed the mores of society. Wherever the early Christians entered a town the power structure got disturbed and immediately sought to convict them for being "disturbers of the peace" and "outside agitators." But they went on with the conviction that they were "a colony of heaven" and had to obey God rather than man. They were small in number but big in commitment. They were too God-intoxicated to be "astronomically intimidated." They brought an end to such ancient evils as infanticide and gladiatorial contest.

Things are different now. The contemporary church is so often a weak, ineffectual voice with an uncertain sound. It is so often the arch supporter of the status quo. Far from being disturbed by the presence of the church, the power structure of the average community is consoled by the church's often vocal sanction of things as they are.

But the judgment of God is upon the church as never before. If the church of today does not recapture the sacrificial spirit of the early church, it will lose its authentic ring, forfeit the loyalty of millions, and be dismissed as an irrelevant social club with no meaning for the twentieth century. I meet young people every day whose disappointment with the church has risen to outright disgust.

I hope the church as a whole will meet the challenge of this decisive hour. But even if the church does not come to the aid of justice, I have no despair about the future. I have no fear about the outcome of our struggle in Birmingham, even if our motives are presently misunderstood. We will reach the goal of freedom in Birmingham and all over the nation, because the goal of America is freedom. Abused and scorned though we may be, our destiny is tied up with the destiny of America. Before the Pilgrims landed at Plymouth, we were here. Before the pen of Jefferson scratched across the pages of history the majestic word of the Declaration of Independence, we were here. For more than two centuries our foreparents labored here without wages; they made cotton king; and they built the homes of their masters in the midst of brutal injustice and shameful humiliation—and yet out of a bottomless vitality our people continue to thrive and develop. If the inexpressible cruelties of slavery could not stop us, the opposition we now face will surely fail. We will win our feedom because the sacred heritage of our nation and the eternal will of God are embodied in our echoing demands.

I must close now. But before closing I am impelled to mention one other point in your statement that troubled me profoundly. You warmly commended the Birmingham police force for keeping "order" and "preventing violence." I don't believe you would have so warmly commended the police force if you had seen its angry violent dogs literally biting six unarmed, nonviolent Negroes. I don't believe you would so quickly commend the policemen if you would observe their ugly and inhuman treatment of Negroes here in the city jail; if you would watch them push and curse old Negro women and young Negro girls; if you would see them slap and kick old Negro men and young boys; if you would observe them, as they did on two occasions, refusing to give us food because we wanted to sing our grace together. I'm sorry that I can't join you in your praise for the police department.

It is true that they have been rather disciplined in their public handling of the demonstrators. In this sense they have been publicly "nonviolent." But for what purpose? To preserve the evil system of segregation. Over the last few years I have consistently preached that nonviolence demands that the means we use must be as pure as the ends we seek. So I have tried to make it clear that it is wrong to use immoral means to attain moral ends. But now I must affirm that it is just as wrong, or even more, to use moral means to preserve immoral ends.

I wish you had commended the Negro demonstrators of Birmingham for their sublime courage, their willingness to suffer, and their amazing discipline in the midst of the most inhuman provocation. One day the South will recognize its real heroes. They will be the James Merediths, courageously and with a majestic sense of purpose facing jeering and hostile mobs and the agonizing loneliness that characterizes the life of the pioneer. They will be old, oppressed, battered Negro women, symbolized in a seventy-two-year-old woman of Montgomery, Alabama, who rose up with a sense of dignity and with her people decided not to ride the segregated buses, and responded to one who inquired about her tiredness with ungrammatical profundity, "My feets is tired, but my soul is rested." They will be young high school and college students, young ministers of the gospel and a host of their elders courageously and nonviolently sitting in at lunch counters and willingly going to jail for conscience's sake. One day the South will know that when these disinherited children of God sat down at lunch counters they were in reality standing up for the best in the Amercian dream and the most sacred values in our Judeo-Christian heritage.

Never before have I written a letter this long—or should I say a book? I'm afraid that it is much too long to take your precious time. I can assure you that it would have been much shorter if I had been writing from a comfortable desk, but what else is there to do when you are alone for days in the dull monotony of a narrow jail cell other than write long letters, think strange thoughts, and pray long prayers?

If I have said anything in this letter that is an understatement of the truth and is indicative of an unreasonable impatience, I beg you to forgive me. If I have said anything in this letter that is an overstatement of the truth and is indicative of my having a patience that makes me patient with anything less than brotherhood, I beg God to forgive me.

Yours for the cause of Peace and Brotherhood,
MARTIN LUTHER KING, JR.

GEORGIA O'KEEFFE
1976

A writer of diverse talents, Joan Didion is the author of five novels, including *Play It as It Lays* (1970), *Democracy* (1977), and *The Last Thing He Wanted* (1997). She has collaborated on screenplays with her husband, novelist John Gregory Dunne; analyzed the social and political turmoil of Latin America in her 1983 book *Salvador;* and offered insights into changing social conditions in the United States through her much-praised investigative reporting and several essay collections. "Georgia O'Keeffe" is a response to a museum exhibition that, like much of Didion's prose, takes the reader beyond its ostensible subject into more complex areas: the nature of identity, portraiture, modern gender relations, and artistic achievement. "Georgia O'Keeffe" is from Didion's 1979 collection of essays, *The White Album.*

"WHERE I WAS BORN and where and how I have lived is unimportant," Georgia O'Keeffe told us in the book of paintings and words published in her ninetieth year on earth. She seemed to be advising us to forget the beautiful face in the Stieglitz photographs. She appeared to be dismissing the rather condescending romance that had attached to her by then, the romance of extreme good looks and advanced age and deliberate isolation. "It is what I have done with where I have been that should be of interest." I recall an August afternoon in Chicago in 1973 when I took my daughter, then seven, to see what Georgia O'Keeffe had done with where she had been. One of the vast O'Keeffe "Sky Above Clouds" canvases floated over the back stairs in the Chicago Art Institute that day, dominating what seemed to be several stories of empty light, and my daughter looked at it once, ran to the landing, and kept on looking. "Who drew it," she whispered after a while. I told her. "I need to talk to her," she said finally.

My daughter was making, that day in Chicago, an entirely unconscious but quite basic assumption about people and the work they do. She was assuming that the glory she saw in the work reflected a glory in its maker, that the painting was the painter as the poem is the poet, that every choice one made alone—every word chosen or rejected, every brush stroke laid or not laid down—betrayed one's character. *Style is character.* It seemed to me that afternoon that I had rarely seen so instinctive an application of this familiar principle, and I recall being pleased not only that my daughter responded to style as character but that it was Georgia O'Keeffe's particular style to which she responded: this was a hard woman who had imposed her 192 square feet of clouds on Chicago.

"Hardness" has not been in our century a quality much admired in women, nor in the past twenty years has it even been in official favor for men. When hardness surfaces in the very old we tend to transform it into "crustiness" or eccentricity, some tonic pepperiness to be indulged at a distance. On the evidence of her work and what she has said about it, Georgia O'Keeffe is neither "crusty" nor eccentric. She is simply hard, a straight shooter, a woman clean of received wisdom and open to what she sees. This is a woman who could early on dismiss most of her contemporaries as "dreamy," and would later single out one she liked as "a very poor painter." (And then add, apparently by way of softening the judgment: "I guess he wasn't a painter at all. He had no courage and I believe that to create one's own world in any of the arts takes courage.") This is a woman who in 1939 could advise her admirers that they were missing her point, that their appreciation of her famous flowers was merely sentimental. "When I paint a red hill," she observed coolly in the catalogue for an exhibition that year, "you say it is too bad that I don't always paint flowers. A flower touches almost everyone's heart. A red hill doesn't touch everyone's heart." This is a woman who could describe the genesis of one of her most well-known paintings—the "Cow's Skull: Red, White and Blue" owned by the Metropolitan—as an act of quite deliberate and derisive orneriness. "I thought of the city men I had been seeing in the East," she wrote. "They talked so often of writing the Great American Novel—the Great American Play—the Great American Poetry. . . . So as I was painting my cow's head on blue I thought to myself, 'I'll make it an American painting. They will not think it great with the red stripes down the sides—Red, White and Blue—but they will notice it.'"

The city men. The men. They. The words crop up again and again as this astonishingly aggressive woman tells us what was on her mind when she was making her astonishingly aggressive paintings. It was those city men who stood accused of sentimentalizing her flowers: "I made you take time to look at what I saw and when you took time to really notice my flower you hung all your associations with flowers on my flower and you write about my flower as if I think and see what you think and see—and I don't." *And I don't.* Imagine those words spoken, and the sound you hear is *don't tread on me.* "The men" believed it impossible to paint New York, so Georgia O'Keeffe painted New York. "The men" didn't think much of her bright color, so she made it brighter. The men yearned toward Europe so she went to Texas, and then New Mexico. The men talked about Cézanne, "long involved remarks about the 'plastic quality' of his form and color," and took one another's long involved remarks, in the view of this angelic rattlesnake in their midst, altogether too seriously. "I can paint one of those dismal-colored paintings like the men," the woman who regarded herself always as an outsider remembers thinking one day in 1922, and she did: a painting of a shed "all low-toned and dreary with the tree beside the door." She called this act of rancor "The Shanty" and hung it in her next show. "The men seemed to approve of it," she reported fifty-four years later, her contempt undimmed. "They seemed to think that maybe I was beginning to paint. That was my only low-toned dismal-colored painting."

Some women fight and others do not. Like so many successful guerrillas in the war between the sexes, Georgia O'Keeffe seems to have been equipped early with an immutable sense of who she was and a fairly clear understanding that she would be required to prove it. On the surface her upbringing was conventional. She was a child on the Wisconsin prairie who played with china dolls and painted watercolors with cloudy skies because sunlight was too hard to paint and, with her brother and sisters, listened every night to her mother read stories of the Wild West, of Texas, of Kit Carson and Billy the Kid. She told adults that she wanted to be an artist and was embarrassed when they asked what kind of artist she wanted to be: she had no idea "what kind." She had no idea what artists did. She had never seen a picture that interested her, other than a pen-and-ink Maid of Athens in one of her mother's books, some Mother Goose illustrations printed on cloth, a tablet cover that showed a little girl with pink roses, and the painting of Arabs on horseback that hung in her grandmother's parlor. At thirteen, in a Dominican convent, she was mortified when the sister corrected her drawing. At Chatham Episcopal Institute in Virginia she painted lilacs and sneaked time alone to walk out to where she could see the line of the Blue Ridge Mountains on the horizon. At the Art Institute in Chicago she was shocked by the presence of live models and wanted to abandon anatomy lessons. At the Art Students League in New York one of her fellow students advised her that, since he would be a great painter and she would end up teaching painting in a girls' school, any work of hers was less important than modeling for him. Another painted over her work to show her how the Impressionists did trees. She had not before heard how the Impressionists did trees and she did not much care.

At twenty-four she left all those opinions behind and went for the first time to live in Texas, where there were no trees to paint and no one to tell her how not to paint them. In Texas there was only the horizon she craved. In Texas she had her sister Claudia with her for a while, and in the late afternoons they would walk away from town and toward the horizon and watch the evening star come out. "That evening star fascinated me," she wrote. "It was in some way very exciting to me. My sister had a gun, and as we walked she would throw bottles into the air and shoot as many as she could before they hit the ground. I had nothing but to walk into nowhere and the wide sunset space with the star. Ten watercolors were made from that star." In a way one's interest is compelled as much by the sister Claudia with the gun as by the painter Georgia with the star, but only the painter left us this shining record. Ten watercolors were made from that star.

THE COWBOY AND HIS COW
1985

Courting controversy was a way of life for Edward Abbey, an environmental activist and prolific writer. The author of the novels *The Monkey Wrench Gang* (1975) and *The Fool's Progress* (1988) chose his enemies with a joyful disregard for personal consequences. But it was a calculated aggressiveness and deeply felt concern for the American landscape that Abbey displayed in his fiction, essays, and speeches. "The Cowboy and His Cow," a speech delivered at the University of Montana in 1985 and reprinted in his essay collection *One Life at a Time, Please,* is vintage Abbey in several respects: both meditative and breathtakingly blunt, alternately personal and polemical, colloquial and analytical. In an age of oratory designed to offend no one and say nothing, Abbey operated from a different frame of mind entirely. Lest anyone assume that his audience's reaction was passive or polite, he included the catcalls and other raucous interjections in the printed version of the speech.

~

W HEN I FIRST CAME WEST in 1948, a student at the University of New Mexico, I was only twenty years old and just out of the Army. I thought, like most simple-minded Easterners, that a cowboy was a kind of mythic hero. I idolized those scrawny little red-nosed hired hands in their tight jeans, funny boots and comical hats.

Like other new arrivals in the West, I could imagine nothing more romantic than becoming a cowboy. Nothing more glorious than owning my own little genuine working cattle outfit. About the only thing better, I thought, was to be a big-league baseball player. I never dreamed that I'd eventually sink to writing books for a living. Unluckily for me—coming from an Appalachian hillbilly background and with a poor choice of parents—I didn't have much money. My father was a small-time logger. He ran a one-man sawmill and a submarginal side-hill farm. There wasn't any money in our family, no inheritance you could run ten thousand cattle on. I had no trust fund to back me up. No Hollywood movie deals to finance a land acquisition program. I lived on what in those days was called the GI Bill, which paid about $150 a month while I went to school. I made that last as long as I could—five or six years. I couldn't afford a horse. The best I could do in 1947 and '48 was buy a third-hand Chevy sedan and roam the West, mostly the Southwest, on holidays and weekends.

I had a roommate at the University of New Mexico. I'll call him Mac. He came from a little town in southwest New Mexico where his father ran a feed store. Mackie was a fair bronc rider, eager to get into the cattle-growing business. And he had some money, enough to buy a little cinderblock house and about forty acres in the Sandia Mountains east of Albuquerque, near a town we called Landfill. Mackie fenced those forty acres, built a corral and kept a few horses there, including an occasional genuine bronco for fun and practice.

I don't remember exactly how Mackie and I became friends in the first place. I was majoring in classical philosophy. He was majoring in screw-worm management. But we got to know each other through the mutual pursuit of a pair of nearly inseparable Kappa Kappa Gamma girls. I lived with him in his little cinderblock house. Helped him meet the mortgage payments. Helped him meet the girls. We were both crude, shy, ugly, obnoxious—like most college boys.

[*Interjection: "Like you!"*]

My friend Mac also owned a 1947 black Lincoln convertible, the kind with the big grille in front, like a cowcatcher on a locomotive, chrome-plated. We used to race to classes in the morning, driving the twenty miles from his house to the campus in never more than fifteen minutes. Usually Mac was too hung over to drive, so I'd operate the car, clutching the wheel while Mac sat beside me waving his big .44, taking potshots at jackrabbits and road signs and billboards and beer bottles. Trying to wake up in time for his ten o'clock class in brand inspection.

I'm sorry to say that my friend Mac was a little bit gun-happy. Most of his forty acres was in tumbleweed. He fenced in about half an acre with chicken wire and stocked that little pasture with white rabbits. He used it as a target range. Not what you'd call sporting, I suppose, but we did eat the rabbits. Sometimes we even went deer hunting with handguns. Mackie with his revolver, and me with a chrome-plated Colt .45 automatic I had liberated from the US Army over in Italy. Surplus government property.

On one of our deer-hunting expeditions, I was sitting on a log in a big clearing in the woods, thinking about Plato and Aristotle and the Kappa Kappa Gamma girls. I didn't really care whether we got a deer that day or not. It was a couple of days before opening, anyway. The whole procedure was probably illegal as hell. Mac was out in the woods somewhere looking for deer around the clearing. I was sitting on the log, thinking, when I saw a chip of bark fly away from the log all by itself, about a foot from my left hand. Then I heard the blast of Mac's revolver—that big old .44 he'd probably liberated from his father. Then I heard him laugh.

"That's not very funny, Mackie," I said.

"Now don't whine and complain, Ed," he said. "You want to be a real hunter like me, you gotta learn to stay awake."

We never did get a deer with handguns. But that's when I had my first little doubts about Mackie, and about the cowboy type in general. But I still loved him. Worshipped him, in fact. I was caught in the grip of the Western myth. Anybody said a word to me about cowboys, I'd jump down his throat with my spurs on. Especially if Mac was standing nearby.

Sometimes I'd try to ride those broncs that he brought in, trying to prove that I could be a cowboy too. Trying to prove it more to myself than to him. I'd be on this crazy, crackpot horse going up, down, left, right and inside out. Hanging on to the saddle horn with both hands. While Mac sat on the corral fence, throwing beer bottles at us and laughing. Every time I got thrown off, Mac would say, "Now get right back on there, Ed. Quick, quick. Don't spoil 'im."

It took me a long time to realize I didn't have to do that kind of work. And it took me another thirty years to realize that there's something wrong at the heart of our most popular American myth—the cowboy and his cow.

[*Jeers.*]

You may have guessed by now that I'm thinking of criticizing the livestock industry. And you are correct. I've been thinking about cows and sheep for many years. Getting more and more disgusted with the whole business. Western cattlemen are nothing more than welfare parasites. They've been getting a free ride on the public lands for over a century, and I think it's time we phased it out. I'm in favor of putting the public-lands livestock grazers out of business.

First of all, we don't need the public-lands beef industry. Even beef lovers don't need it. According to most government reports (Bureau of Land Management, Forest Service), only about 2 percent of our beef, our red meat, comes from the public lands of the eleven Western states. By those eleven I mean Montana, Nevada, Utah, Colorado, New Mexico, Arizona, Idaho, Wyoming, Oregon, Washington and California. Most of our beef, aside from imports, comes from the Midwest and the East, especially the Southeast—Georgia, Alabama, Florida—and from other private lands across the nation. More beef cattle are raised in the state of Georgia than in the sagebrush empire of Nevada. And for a very good reason: back East, you can support a cow on maybe half an acre. Out here, it takes anywhere from twenty-five to fifty acres. In the red-rock country of Utah, the rule of thumb is one section—a square mile—per cow.

[*Shouts from rear of hall.*]

Since such a small percentage of cows are produced on public lands in the West, eliminating that part of the industry should not raise supermarket beef prices very much. Furthermore, we'd save money in the taxes we now pay for various subsidies to these public-lands cattlemen. Subsidies for things like "range improvement"—tree chaining, sagebrush clearing, mesquite poisoning, disease control, predator trapping, fencing, wells, stockponds, roads. Then there are the salaries of those who work for government agencies like the Bureau of Land Management (BLM) and the Forest Service. You could probably also count in a big part of the salaries of the overpaid professors engaged in range-management research at the Western land-grant colleges.

Moreover, the cattle have done, and are doing, intolerable damage to our public lands—our national forests, state lands, BLM-administered lands, wildlife preserves, even some of our national parks and monuments. In Utah's Capital Reef National Park, for example, grazing is still allowed. In fact, it's recently been extended for another ten years, and Utah politicians are trying to make the arrangement permanent. They probably won't get away with it. But there we have at least one case where cattle are still tramping about in a national park, transforming soil and grass into dust and weeds.

[*Disturbance.*]

Overgrazing is much too weak a term. Most of the public lands in the West and especially in the Southwest, are what you might call "cowburnt." Almost anywhere and everywhere you go in the American West you find hordes of these ugly, clumsy, stupid, bawling, stinking, fly-covered, shit-smeared, disease-spreading brutes. They are a pest and a plague. They pollute our springs and streams and rivers. They infest our canyons, valleys, meadows and forests. They graze off the native bluestem and grama and bunch grasses, leaving behind jungles of prickly pear. They trample down the native forbs and shrubs and cacti. They spread the exotic cheatgrass, the Russian thistle and the crested wheat grass. *Weeds.*

Even when the cattle are not physically present, you'll see the dung and the flies and the mud and the dust and the general destruction. If you don't see it, you'll smell it. The whole American West stinks of cattle. Along every flowing stream, around every seep and spring and water hole and well, you'll find acres and acres of what range-management specialists call "sacrifice areas"—another understatement. These are places denuded of forage, except for some cactus or a little tumbleweed or maybe a few mutilated trees like mesquite, juniper or hackberry.

I'm not going to bonmbard you with graphs and statistics, which don't make much of an impression on intelligent people anyway. Anyone who goes beyond the city limits of almost any Western town can see for himself that the land is overgrazed. There are too many cows and horses and sheep out there. Of course, cattlemen would never publicly confess to overgrazing, any more than Dracula would publicly confess to a fondness for blood. Cattlemen are interested parties. Many of them will not give reliable testimony. Some have too much at stake: their Cadillacs and their airplanes, their ranch resale profits and their capital gains. (I'm talking about the corporation ranchers, the land-and-cattle companies, the investment syndicates.) Others, those ranchers who have only a small base property, flood the public lands with their cows. About 8 percent of the federal land permittees have cattle that consume approximately 45 percent of the forage on the government rangelands.

Beef ranchers like to claim that their cows do not compete with deer. Deer are browsers, cows are grazers. That's true. But when a range is overgrazed, when the grass is gone (as it often is for seasons at a time), then cattle become browsers too, out of necessity. In the Southwest, cattle commonly feed on mesquite, cliff rose, cactus, acacia or any other shrub or tree they find biodegradable. To that extent they compete with deer. And they tend to drive out other and better wildlife. Like elk, or bighorn sheep, or pronghorn antelope.

[*Sneers, jeers, laughter.*]

How much damage have cattle done to the Western rangelands? Large-scale beef ranching has been going on since the 1870s. There's plenty of documentation of the effects of this massive cattle grazing on the erosion of the land, the character of the land, the character of the vegetation. Streams and rivers that used to flow on the surface all year round are now intermittent, or underground, because of overgrazing and rapid runoff.

Our public lands have been overgrazed for a century. The BLM knows it; the Forest Service knows it. The Government Accounting Office knows it. And overgrazing means eventual ruin, just like stripmining or clear-cutting or the damming of rivers. Much of the Southwest already looks like Mexico or southern Italy or North Africa: a cowburnt wasteland. As we destroy our land, we destroy our agricultural economy and the basis of modern society. If we keep it up, we'll gradually degrade American life to the status of life in places like Mexico or southern Italy or Libya or Egypt.

In 1984 the Bureau of Land Management, which was required by Congress to report on its stewardship of our rangelands—the property of all Americans, remember—confessed that 31 percent of the land it administered was in "good condition," and 60 percent in "poor condition." And it reported that only 18 percent of the rangelands were improving, while 68 percent were "stable" and 14 percent were getting worse. If the BLM said that, we can safely assume that range conditions are actually much worse.

[*Shouts of "bullshit!"*]

What can we do about this situation? This is the fun part— this is the part I like. It's not easy to argue that we should do away with cattle ranching. The cowboy myth gets in the way. But I do have some solutions to overgrazing.

[*A yell: "Cowboys do it better!" Answered by another: "Ask any cow!" Coarse laughter.*]

I'd begin by reducing the number of cattle on public lands. Not that range managers would go along with it, of course. In their eyes, and in the eyes of the livestock associations they work for, cutting down on the number of cattle is the worst possible solution—an impossible solution. So they propose all kinds of gimmicks. Portable fencing and perpetual movement of cattle. More cross-fencing. More wells and ponds so that more land can be exploited. These proposals are basically a maneuver by the Forest Service and the BLM to appease their critics without offending their real bosses in the beef industry. But a drastic reduction in cattle numbers is the only true and honest solution.

I also suggest that we open a hunting season on range cattle. I realize that beef cattle will not make sporting prey at first. Like all domesticated animals (including most humans), beef cattle are slow, stupid and awkward. But the breed will improve if hunted regularly. And as the number of cattle is reduced, other and far more useful, beautiful and interesting animals will return to the rangelands and will increase.

Suppose, by some miracle of Hollywood or inheritance or good luck, I should acquire a respectable-sized working cattle outfit. What would I do with it? First, I'd get rid of the stinking, filthy cattle. Every single animal. Shoot them all, and stock the place with real animals, real game, real protein: elk, buffalo, pronghorn antelope, bighorn sheep, moose. And some purely decorative animals, like eagles. We need more eagles. And wolves. We need more wolves. Mountain lions and bears. Especially, of course, grizzly bears. Down in the desert, I would stock every water tank, every water hole, every stockpond, with alligators.

You may note that I have said little about coyotes or deer. Coyotes seem to be doing all right on their own. They're smarter than their enemies. I've never heard of a coyote as dumb as a sheepman. As for deer, especially mule deer, they, too, are surviving—maybe even thriving, as some game and fish departments claim, though nobody claims there are as many deer now as there were before the cattle industry was introduced in the West. In any case, compared to elk the deer is a second-rate game animal, nothing but a giant rodent—a rat with antlers.

[*Portions of audience begin to leave.*]

I've suggested that the beef industry's abuse of our Western lands is based on the old mythology of the cowboy as natural nobleman. I'd like to conclude this diatribe with a few remarks about this most cherished and fanciful of American fairy tales. In truth, the cowboy is only a hired hand. A farm boy in leather britches and a comical hat. A herdsman who gets on a horse to do part of his work. Some ranchers are also cowboys, but most are not. There is a difference. There are many ranchers out there who are big-time farmers of the public lands—our property. As such, they do not merit any special consideration or special privileges. There are only about 31,000 ranchers in the whole American West who use the public lands. That's less than the population of Missoula, Montana.

The rancher (with a few honorable exceptions) is a man who strings barbed wire all over the range; drills wells and bulldozes stockponds; drives off elk and antelope and bighorn sheep; poisons coyotes and prairie dogs; shoots eagles, bears and cougars on sight; supplants the native grasses with tumbleweed, snakeweed, povertyweed, cowshit, anthills, mud, dust and flies. And then leans back and grins at the TV cameras and talks about how much he loves the American West. Cowboys also are greatly overrated. Consider the nature of their work. Suppose you had to spend most of your working hours sitting on a horse, contemplating the hind end of a cow. How would that affect your imagination? Think what it does to the relatively simple mind of the average peasant boy, raised amid the bawling of calves and cows in the splatter of mud and the stink of shit.

[*Shouting. Laughter. Disturbance.*]

Do cowboys work hard? Sometimes. But most ranchers don't work very hard. They have a lot of leisure time for politics and bellyaching (which is why most state legislatures in the West are occupied and dominated by cattlemen). Anytime you go into a small Western town you'll find them at the nearest drugstore, sitting around all morning drinking coffee, talking about their tax breaks.

Is a cowboy's work socially useful? No. As I've already pointed out, subsidized Western range beef is a trivial item in the national beef economy. If all of our 31,000 Western public-land ranchers quit tomorrow, we'd never even notice. Any public school teacher does harder work, more difficult work, more dangerous work and far more valuable work than the cowboy or rancher. The same thing applies to registered nurses and nurses' aides, garbage collectors and traffic cops. Harder work, tougher work, more necessary work. We need those people in our complicated society. We do not need cowboys or ranchers. We've carried them on our backs long enough.

[*Disturbance in rear of hall.*]

"This Abbey," the cowboys and their lovers will say, "this

Abbey is a wimp. A chicken-hearted sentimentalist with no feel for the hard realities of practical life." Especially critical of my attitude will be the Easterners and Midwesterners newly arrived here from their Upper West Side apartments, their rustic lodges in upper Michigan. Our nouveau Westerners with their toy ranches, their pickup trucks with the gun racks, their pointy-toed boots with the undershot heels, their gigantic hats. And, of course, their pet horses. The *instant rednecks*.

[*Shouts.*]

To those who might accuse me of wimpery and sentimentality, I'd like to say this in reply. I respect real men. I admire true manliness. But I despise arrogance and brutality and bullies. So let me close with some nice remarks about cowboys and cattle ranchers. They are a mixed lot, like the rest of us. As individuals, they range from the bad to the ordinary to the good. A rancher, after all, is only a farmer, cropping the public rangelands with his four-legged lawnmowers, stashing our grass into his bank account. A cowboy is a hired hand trying to make an honest living. Nothing special.

I have no quarrel with these people as fellow humans. All I want to do is get their cows off our property. Let those cowboys and ranchers find some harder way to make a living, like the rest of us have to do. There's no good reason why we should subsidize them forever. They've had their free ride. It's time they learned to support themselves.

In the meantime, I'm going to say good-bye to all you cowboys and cowgirls. I love the legend too—but keep your sacred cows and your dead horses out of my elk pastures.

[*Sitting ovation. Gunfire in parking lot.*]

Leo Marx

HUCK AT 100
1985

A teacher for many years at M.I.T. and Amherst College and author of *The Machine in the Garden,* Leo Marx was one of the founders of the academic discipline known as American Studies. An authority on nineteenth-century American literature, he has also written extensively on the paradoxical role of technology in modern life and the Western fascination with scientific progress. In "Huck at 100," published in *The Nation* in 1985, Marx addresses one of the most difficult controversies of the culture wars in late twentieth-century America: how is a society equally opposed to censorship and racism to deal with controversial and variously interpreted novels like Mark Twain's *Huckleberry Finn?*

E VER SINCE IT WAS PUBLISHED, exactly one hundred years ago, Mark Twain's *Adventures of Huckleberry Finn* has been a target of moral disapproval. Many of the novel's first reviewers found it disturbing and offensive. They called it, among other things, vulgar, inelegant, ungrammatical, coarse, irreverent, semiobscene, trashy and vicious. The library in Concord, Massachusetts, promptly banned it, but the book soon won the affection of a large audience, and during the next fifty years critics, scholars and writers succeeded in rescuing it from the mincingly refined standards of what George Santayana aptly named "the genteel tradition." In the 1930s Ernest Hemingway praised *Huckleberry Finn* as the work from which all modern American writing stems, and T. S. Eliot later described Mark Twain's vernacular style as nothing less than "a new discovery in the English language." By the 1950s the initial objections to the novel had been dispelled, and it was quietly installed, along with *The Scarlet Letter* and some other "classic"

American books, in the more or less standard high-school English curriculum.

But then, having survived the disdain of the genteel critics, the book became the object of another, angrier and more damaging kind of moral condemnation. In 1957 the National Association for the Advancement of Colored People called *Huckleberry Finn* racially offensive, and since then we have seen a mounting protest against this novel whose first-person narrator, the fourteen-year-old son of the town drunk, routinely refers to blacks as "niggers." Huck's repeated use of that demeaning epithet is enough to convince many black Americans that schoolchildren should not be required to read the book. (Another, somewhat less obvious reason for their disquiet is a certain resemblance between the novel's leading black character, the escaped slave, Jim, and the stereotypical minstrel-show darkie.) In the last few years the protest has been gaining adherents. In a number of cities across the country, indignant parents, educators and school-board members have demanded that the book be removed from the curriculum and even, in some instances, that it be banned from school or public libraries. This past year a group of black parents succeeded in having the novel taken off the list of required reading in Waukegan, Illinois, and John H. Wallace, an educator with the school board in Chicago, is now conducting a nationwide campaign against Mark Twain's greatest work, which he calls "the most grotesque example of racist trash ever written."

One result of this protest is that the centenary of *Huckleberry Finn* has been marked by a curious conjunction of celebration and denunciation. In March, when Shelley Fisher Fishkin, a literary scholar at Yale University, came to Mark Twain's defense, she attracted national attention to the dispute about his racial views. In an announcement treated as front-page news by *The New York Times,* she reported the authentication of an 1885 letter in which Twain offered to provide financial support for a black student at Yale Law School. There he wrote that "we have ground the manhood out of . . . [black men] & the shame is ours, not theirs; and we should pay for it." (He subsequently did provide the money.) Because the letter reveals "the personal anguish that Twain felt regarding the destructive legacy of slavery," Fishkin evidently thought that it might help to overcome the objections of black people to *Huckleberry Finn.* The implication was that a man of such enlightened views could not possibly have written a racially offensive novel and that once those views were established, the controversy would be resolved.

But as it turned out, the Yale letter merely provoked the contending parties to recast their arguments in less compromising, more strident language. Thus Sterling Stuckey, a historian at Northwestern University who is black, was moved to reaffirm the received scholarly-critical estimate of Mark Twain's masterwork. Of the letter he said that it "couldn't be a clearer, more categorical indictment of racism in American life," and he went on to praise *Huckleberry Finn* as "one of the most devastating attacks on racism ever written." But Wallace, perhaps the novel's most outspoken critic, was unmoved by Fishkin's announcement. When asked to comment on the new evidence of Mark Twain's sympathy for blacks, he said that it "still does not mitigate the problems that children have with *Huck Finn.* . . . The book teaches blatant racism. . . . We ought to get it off the school reading list."

What shall we make of this unusual controversy? Unlike most issues of public policy involving opposed literary judgments, the current argument about the place of *Huckleberry Finn* in the public school curriculum does not involve censorship or First Amendment rights. Whether or not high-school students are required to read a particular novel has nothing to do with anyone's freedom of speech. (I am putting aside the very different and, to my mind, intolerable proposal to remove the book from school or public libraries.) Another striking feature of the dispute is the extremity of the antagonists' views. Most public quarrels about the merit of literary works turn on relatively subtle questions of interpretation, but in this case an enormous gulf separates those who consider *Huckleberry Finn* to be "one of the most devastating attacks on racism ever written" from those who denounce it as "racist trash"—who claim that it actually "teaches" blatant racism. At first sight, indeed, the two parties seem to be so far apart as to make the controversy irresolvable, and perhaps it is. But it may be useful, as a step toward a resolution, to consider why this novel lends itself to such antithetical readings. How is it possible for *Huckleberry Finn* to convey such diametrically opposed attitudes toward American racism?

The explanation should begin, I think, with a decisive though perhaps insufficiently appreciated fact: the racial attitudes to which this novel lends overt expression are not Mark Twain's, they are those of an ignorant adolescent boy. This fact also explains, incidentally, why evidence from other sources about what the writer, Samuel L. Clemens, may have thought or said on the subject of race (as in the Yale letter) proves to be largely beside the point. That a considerable disparity often exists between what writers believe and what their work conveys is an axiom of modern criticism. In the case of a first-person narrative like *Huckleberry Finn,* of course, Clemens's viewpoint is manifestly disguised, and can only make itself felt obliquely, in the voice of—from behind the mask of—the boy narrator, Huck.

In accounting for the ability of readers to arrive at radically opposed conclusions about the racial attitudes embodied in this novel, the importance of the first-person narrative method cannot be exaggerated. Every word, every thought, every perception, emanates from Huck or, in passages where other characters speak, is reported by him—filtered through his mind. *Adventures of Huckleberry Finn* is a tour de force of sustained impersonation. It is a tale told by a boy who is a vagrant and a virtual outcast, who has no mother (she is never mentioned), whose father is an illiterate drunk, bigot and bully, and who is inclined to accept society's view of people like himself as being, in his own words, irremediably "wicked and low-down and ornery."

Of course Huck calls black people "niggers"; for him to refer to them any other way would be inconceivable. But to say this can be misleading if it is taken to imply that the difficulty comes down to a mere question of usage, as if Mark Twain might have absolved his narrator (and himself) of the charge of racism merely by cleaning up Huck's vocabulary. The truth is that *Huckleberry Finn* is written from the viewpoint of a racist, or, to be more precise, a semiracist—a racist with a difference. The difference stems in part from Huck's exceptionally empathic nature (or, as Mark Twain puts it, his "sound heart") and in part from his disreputable upbringing on the fringe of antebellum Southern society. Unlike Tom Sawyer and his other friends whose parents belong to "the quality," Huck has been spared much of the formative influence of family, church and school. His racial prejudice is not supported by a sense of family or social superiority. On the contrary, he is a distinct outsider, a boy who is only half "civilized" or, in social science idiom, he has been incompletely acculturated. Although he has picked up the received version of white racism along with other bits and pieces of the dominant belief system, that viewpoint has been less deeply implanted in him than in respectable children like Tom Sawyer.

In moments of crisis, accordingly, Huck comes up against the discrepancy between the standard conception of black people as "niggers"—a conception he shares—and what he has learned as a result of his direct experience with Jim. During such crises his inner struggle characteristically begins with an unquestioning endorsement of the culture's stock prejudices, but then, when he tries to enact them, he balks and, in consequence, he inadvertently reveals their inhumanity. When, for example, it suddenly occurs to him that his journey with an escaped slave will determine what people back home think about him, his first reaction is wholly conventional: "It would get all around that Huck Finn helped a nigger to get his freedom; and if I was ever to see anybody from that town again, I'd be ready to get down and lick his boots for shame." He knows what he is supposed to do if he wants the respect of law-abiding citizens, but the thought of turning Jim in calls up vivid memories of Jim's loyalty and friendship, and he finally decides that he can't do it; he would rather go to hell. The conflict between Huck's stock racist ideas and his compassionate nature exemplifies the way the controlling irony works: when he thinks he is behaving ignobly, we are invited to recognize his innate nobility. What makes the outcome so powerful is that the novel's readers are compelled to effect the ironic reversal. That Huck can acknowledge Jim's humanity only by violating the moral code of a racist society is an implication that the boy is unable to grasp or put into words. It is a thought that Mark Twain's readers must formulate for themselves.

But of course the centrality of that irony also explains why some readers consider *Huckleberry Finn* a racist book. For whatever reason, and one can imagine several, they mistake the hero's flagrant if erratic racism for the novel's—the author's—viewpoint. It may be difficult, admittedly, for admirers of this wonderful book to believe that an average, reasonably competent reader could fail to recognize that its satirical thrust is directed against slavery and racial bigotry, but it does happen. Leaving aside the incontrovertible evidence that some adult readers do miss the point, it must be emphasized that Wallace and those who share his views are not chiefly concerned about the novel's effect on mature, competent readers. They are concerned about its effect on schoolchildren, all schoolchildren, but especially black American children, whose special experience might very well hinder their responsiveness to the ironic treatment of racial oppression. How much do we know, actually, about the ability of teachers, or of children of various ages and social backgrounds, to make sense of ironic discourse? I have taught this book with pleasure to hundreds of college students, but I'm not at all confident about my ability to persuade a class of inner-city adolescents—or any literal-minded adolescents, for that matter—that a book can say, or seem to say, one thing and mean another; or that in this case we should not be troubled by the fact that the hero calls black people "niggers" because, after all, that's what all white Southerners called them back then, and anyway, look, in the end he is loyal to Jim.

And besides, what does one say about Jim? There can be no doubt that Mark Twain wants us to admire him; he is a sympathetic, loving, self-abnegating, even saintly, "Christ-like" man. But what does one tell black children about his extreme passivity, his childlike credulity, his cloying deference toward the white boy? Aren't these the traits of a derisory racial stereotype, the fawning black male? To overcome objections on that score, one would have to stress Jim's cunning and his occasional refusal to play the minstrel darkie, especially the great episode in which he drops his habitual pose of docility, if it is a pose, and angrily denounces Huck for making him the victim of a cruel joke. "It was fifteen minutes," Huck says about his reluctant apology, "before I could work myself up to go and humble myself to a nigger—but I done it, and I warn't ever sorry for it afterwards, neither." It is a splendid moment, but is it splendid enough to offset the inescapable doubts of black readers about Jim's customary pliancy? Is it enough that Jim, the only black male of any significance in the novel, asserts his dignity in this one moving episode?

To raise these complex issues, it need hardly be said, is not to condone the denunciation of the novel as racist trash. But even if that opinion is as wrongheaded as I believe it to be, it does not follow that those who hold it are necessarily wrong about the inappropriateness of requiring high-school teachers to teach, and students to read, the *Adventures of Huckleberry Finn*. The point at issue, then, is the justification for that requirement. To claim that it should be required reading because it is a great American book is unconvincing: we don't require students to read most great books. Objections to the requirement become more understandable if we recognize the unique character of the niche Twain's novel tends to occupy in the high-school English course. It often is the only book that is centrally concerned with racial oppression.

All of which suggests that educators could take a large step toward resolving the current controversy simply by eliminating the requirement. This would open the way for the ideal solution to allow each teacher to decide whether his or her students should be asked to read *Huckleberry Finn*. It is the teachers, after all, who are best qualified to make a sensible and informed decision, one that would rest on their confidence in their own ability to convey, and their students' ability to grasp, the irony that informs every word of this matchless comic novel.

Pico Iyer

IN PRAISE OF THE HUMBLE COMMA
1988

A former staff writer for *Time* magazine and the author of the novel *Cuba and the Night,* Pico Iyer was born in England of Indian parents and educated at Oxford. He has lived most of his adult life in California, though his frequent travels have taken him across Asia, Africa, and Europe and been the subject of many of his most widely read essays. A "post-modern traveler," as the *New York Times* has described him, Iyer is a man "rooted nowhere and moving on in order to disprove the illusion of home." Writing about the Himalayas, New York City, contemporary novels, or marks of punctuation, Iyer displays the same strong sense of cadence and metaphor, acute observation and vivid description. His nonfiction books include *Video Night in Kathmandu, The Lady and the Monk, Falling Off the Map,* and *Classical Tropical.*

THE GODS, THEY SAY, GIVE BREATH, and they take it away. But the same could be said—could it not?—of the humble comma. Add it to the present clause and, of a sudden, the mind is, quite literally, given pause to think; take it out if you wish or forget it and the mind is deprived of a resting place. Yet still the comma gets no respect. It seems just a slip of a thing, a pedant's tick, a blip on the edge of our consciousness, a kind of printer's smudge almost. Small, we claim, is beautiful (especially in the age of the microchip). Yet what is so often used, and so rarely recalled, as the comma—unless it be breath itself?

Punctuation, one is taught, has a point: to keep up law and order. Punctuation marks are the road signs placed along the highway of our communication—to control speeds, provide directions, and prevent head-on collisions. A period has the unblinking finality of a red light; the comma is a flashing yellow light that asks us only to slow down; and the semicolon is a Stop sign that tells us to ease gradually to a halt, before gradually starting up again. By establishing the relations between words, punctuation establishes the relations between the people using words. That may be one reason why schoolteachers exalt it, and lovers defy it ("We love each other and belong to each other let's don't ever hurt each other Nicole let's don't ever hurt each other," wrote Gary Gilmore to his girlfriend). A comma, he must have known, "separates inseparables," in the clinching words of H. W. Fowler, king of English Usage.

Punctuation, then, is a civic prop, a pillar that holds society upright. (A run-on sentence, its phrases piling up without division, is as unsightly as a sink piled high with dirty dishes.) Small wonder, then, that punctuation was one of the first proprieties of the Victorian Age, the age of the corset, that the modernists threw off: the sexual revolution might be said to have begun when Joyce's Molly Bloom spilled out all her private thoughts in thirty-six pages of panting, unperioded, and officially censored prose; and another rebellion was surely marked when e. e. cummings first committed "god" to the lower case.

Punctuation thus becomes the signature of cultures. The hot-blooded Spaniard seems to be revealed in the passion and urgency of his doubled exclamation points and question marks ("¡Caramba! ¿Quién sabe?"), while the impassive Chinese traditionally added to his so-called inscrutability by omitting all directions from his ideograms. The anarchy and commotion of the sixties were given voice in the exploding exclamation marks, riotous capital letters, and Day-Glo italics of Tom Wolfe's spray-paint prose; and in Communist societies, where the State is absolute, the dignity—and divinity—of capital letters is reserved for Ministries, Subcommittees and Secretariats.

Yet punctuation is something more than a culture's birthmark; it scores the music in our minds, gets our thoughts moving to the rhythm of our hearts. Punctuation is the notation in the sheet music of our words, telling us when to rest, or when to raise our voices; it acknowledges that the meaning of our discourse, as of any symphonic composition, lies not in the units but in the pauses, the pacing, and the phrasing. Punctuation is the way one bats one's eyes, lowers one's voice, or blushes demurely. Punctuation adjusts color and tone and volume till the feeling comes into perfect focus: not disgust exactly, but distaste; not lust, or like, but love.

Punctuation, in short, gives us the human voice, and all the meanings that lie between the words. "You aren't young, are you?" loses its innocence when it loses the question mark. Every child knows the menace of a dropped apostrophe (the parent's "Don't do that" shifting into the more slowly enunciated "Do not do that") and every believer the ignominy of having his faith reduced to "faith." Add an exclamation point to "To be or not to be . . ." and the gloomy Dane has all the resolve he needs; add a comma, and the noble sobriety of "God save the Queen" becomes a cry of desperation bordering on double sacrilege.

Sometimes, of course, our markings may be simply a matter of aesthetics. Popping in a comma can be like slipping on the necklace that gives an outfit quiet elegance, or like catching the sound of running water that complements, as it completes, the silence of a Japanese landscape. When V. S. Naipaul, in his latest novel, writes, "He was a middle-aged man, with glasses," the first comma can seem a little precious. Yet it gives the description a spin, as well as a subtlety, that it otherwise lacks, and it shows that the glasses are not part of the middle-agedness, but something else.

Thus all these tiny scratches give us breadth and heft and depth. A world that has only periods is a world without inflections. It is a world without shade. It has a music without sharps and flats. It is a martial music. It has a jackboot rhythm. Words cannot bend and curve. A comma, by comparison, catches the gentle drift of the mind in thought, turning in on itself and back on itself, reversing, redoubling, and returning along the course of its own sweet river music; while the semicolon brings clauses and thoughts together with all the silent discretion of a hostess arranging guests around her dinner table.

Punctuation, then, is a matter of care. Care for words, yes, but also, and more important, for what the words imply. Only a lover notices the small things: the way the afternoon light catches the nape of a neck, or how a strand of hair slips out from behind an ear, or the way a finger curls around a cup. And no one scans a letter so closely as a lover, searching for the small print, straining to hear its nuances, its gasps, its sighs and hesitations, poring over the secret messages that lie in every cadence. The difference between "Jane (whom I adore)" and "Jane, whom I adore," and the difference between them both and "Jane—whom I adore," marks all the distance between ecstasy and heartache. "No iron can pierce the heart with such force as a period put at just the right place," in Isaac Babel's lovely words; a comma can let us hear a voice break, or a heart. Punctuation, in fact, is a labor of love. Which brings us back, in a way, to gods.

I. F. Stone

WHEN FREE SPEECH WAS FIRST CONDEMNED: THE TRIAL OF SOCRATES RECONSIDERED
1988

A caustic journalist and passionate defender of civil liberties, I. F. Stone is something of a legend in journalistic circles, and for forty years his publication, *I. F. Stone's Weekly,* was a bible for the political left. Stone's writings were collected in *The Hidden History of the Korean War* (1988), *The Haunted Fifties* (1989), *In a Time of Torment: A Nonconformist History of Our Times* (1989), and other books of social commentary. "When Free Speech was First Condemned" appeared in *Harper's Magazine* in 1988 at the time of the publication of Stone's well-received book about the subject, *The Trial of Socrates.* Appropriately, Stone articulates his views in a form common to the classroom but less frequent on the page: the Socratic dialogue.

~

I N 399 B.C. SOCRATES STOOD TRIAL for impiety and for corrupting the youth of Athens. The speech Socrates made to the 500–man jury, reconstructed by Plato in his *Apology,* is a classic text of Greek philosophy and part of the canon of Western thought. But the speech did not convince the jury of Socrates' innocence: he was sentenced to death by poisoning.

What follows is an analysis of the trial and some thoughts on how it might have gone differently—in particular, how Socrates might have won acquittal. Cast as a dialogue, it presents the struggle to preserve free speech in a context relevant to both the ancient and the modern world.

What is the most important discovery you have made about the trial of Socrates?

How easily he might have won acquittal.

What's your evidence?

To start with, the slim majority who voted for conviction.

What was the vote?

The vote of the jury was 280 for conviction and 220 for acquittal. So a shift of 30 votes—or six percent of the voters—would have created a tie, and in Athens a tie would set free the accused.

Was Socrates aware of this?

Of course. In Plato's *Apology,* he expresses his surprise at the narrowness of the verdict against him. "I did not expect so small a majority," he says, "but a large one."

Why was Socrates surprised?

Socrates clearly expected a large and decisive majority against him. I think he had good reason to be surprised by the close vote. His life-long teaching had been consistently hostile to Athenian democracy, and his thought and opinions had attracted the kind of anti-democratic and pro-Spartan "jet set" youth who had twice overthrown the democracy in the decade and a half before his trial. Moreover, his chief accuser, Anytos, enjoyed great prestige—he was one of the generals who restored democracy in Athens barely four years before Socrates was indicted. If the Athenian demos, the common people or the many, had been as benighted and biased as Socrates believed them to be, his case would indeed have been hopeless. But the closely divided jury shows that his case was not hopeless—that the jury was troubled about convicting him.

Why do you think the jury was troubled?

Because free expression permeated the political and artistic life of Athens and had made it—as Pericles boasts in Thucydides—"the school of Hellas." Philosophers from all over the Mediterranean world flocked to Athens to address its eager audiences. The city had neither a sacred party line nor an un-

Athenian Activities Committee. And what in truth had Socrates done? He denied that he had ever joined in any of the aristocratic conspiracies against the government of Athens or committed any overt act against it, and no evidence was offered to the contrary. He had done his duty bravely as a citizen soldier. He was indicted for what he said and taught: it was purely a prosecution of *ideas,* and therefore at odds with the city's most basic traditions. That is what must have troubled the Athenians then as it still troubles the modern reader now. Indeed, if the Athenians had not felt so strongly about free speech they would not have waited until Socrates was seventy before taking him to court.

So what conclusion do you draw from this?

If Socrates had pleaded the right to free speech, if he had offered a civil-libertarian defense, if he had appealed to the fundamental principles of Athenian democracy, I believe he could have turned that closely divided jury to his favor and won acquittal.

Why didn't he do so?

Socrates didn't believe in free speech and he wanted to be convicted. There is evidence, of which too few are aware, that he wanted to die and set out deliberately to provoke the jury.

So where do you begin your retrial of the case?

With the fundamental divergence between the premises of Athenian democracy and the teachings of Socrates.

How do you describe them?

One might think, from reading Plato, that Socrates became unpopular because he went around exhorting his fellow citizens to virtue. Of course that is one way to lose friends in any society. But there were basic issues about which Socrates differed irreconcilably with his fellow citizens, and indeed with those of all but the most backward Greek areas like Crete and Sparta, or semi-barbarian Macedonia. Socrates was not just anti-democratic. He was anti-political in the Greek sense of the term. He did not approve of the polis, whether ruled by the many, as in the democracies, or the few, as in the oligarchies. He did not believe that people were capable of self-government: he saw the human community as a herd. A herd requires a shepherd as its master, and the herdsman does not consult his sheep.

Socrates rejected the polis altogether. He felt that the good life could only be achieved by withdrawing from it and keeping one's soul unsullied by politics.

What was the dominant Greek view?

Artistotle later summed this up best when he declared that man is a political animal, i.e., an animal that lives in a city-state or community, *koinonia.* Communal life is made possible because man, unlike the other animals, has Logos—the power of reasoned and persuasive speech. He can tell right from wrong, and therefore is able to live peacefully with his fellows with sufficient respect for the opinions and rights of others to make the community viable. Aristotle said that the solitary man is either a savage or a god.

The attaining of knowledge for him, as for most Greeks, was not a metaphysical wild goose chase for unattainable absolute definitions—for that is what Socrates was up to—but the steady accumulation of common wisdom distilled from common experience. Finally, Aristotle saw the city as the place where men could best achieve the good life, each fulfilling his individual capacities, whether as a tragic poet or a humble craftsman, or, yes, as an endless and eternally charming talker like Socrates. Socrates would have died frustrated and unfulfilled without the ever-curious listeners and ready interlocutors Athens afforded him.

Imagine! In Plato's dialogue the *Gorgias,* we find Socrates—who made loquacity his life's mission—accusing Pericles of having made the Athenians talkative!

Are you expressing the views of Socrates, or Plato's view of Socrates' views?

These are views attributed to Socrates in Xenophon as well as Plato; both were disciples of Socrates, and together they provide us with the fullest contemporary view of him. This is also the opinion of other followers of Socrates. His followers varied widely, as St. Augustine notes, in their philosophical views. But politically all Socratics rejected the polis, as Socrates himself did.

Who did Socrates believe should rule?

The ideal, indeed the only rational, ruler for Socrates, as expressed by him in Xenophon's *Memorabilia,* was "the man who knows." This was, of course, the germ that Plato developed into the idea of rule by a philosopher-king.

Did Socrates ever think of running for public office as "the man who knows"?

The Delphic oracle, as Socrates boasted, said that no one was wiser than he. But Socrates spent his life demonstrating that he knew only that he *didn't* know, which put him one rung above all other Athenians, none of whom could meet his standard for real knowledge.

So that left the city up a creek with no qualified candidate?

Exactly.

So Socrates had nothing but contempt for the city-state?

Well, he did have a curious infatuation with Sparta, the great rival and enemy of Athens.

Why do you call it curious?

Because Sparta had no use for a Socrates. It was suspicious of foreigners and foreign ideas. It was a dour military state where members of the ruling class led a barracks existence of constant military training. They were a minority holding down their human herd of serfs, the helots, who cultivated their fields. Traders and craftsmen, members of the middle class—which in Athens was the most dynamic element in society—led a stunted

and barely tolerated existence on the fringes of Spartan life, and
were denied the rights of citizenship. Sparta was devoid of
philosophers and artists. It never had a Parthenon or a theater. It
had one or two poets, but these were famous mostly for war
songs. Sparta and Crete were the cultural deserts of ancient
Greece. Yet we know from Plato's *Crito* that Socrates admired
these tight little militaristic oligarchies. Just why is never
explained.

Did such crotchety views bother the Athenians?

Yes, because the idealization of Sparta was characteristic of
the young, wealthy, disaffected aristocrats who hated democracy
and were both contemptuous and envious of the "pushy" traders
and craftsmen who were achieving wealth and contesting the
political primacy of the old landed gentry. Socrates, though
himself middle class (the son of a stonecutter), became the idol
of the disdainful and alienated young aristocrats in Athens,
Plato and Xenophon among them.

How do we know this?

From our earliest contemporary glimpse of Socratic politics:
the *Birds* of Aristophanes. In a joyous spoof of his fellow
Athenians, the comic poet ridiculed these privileged young mal-
contents for imitating Spartan manners, wearing their hair long
and unkempt, going around unwashed, wearing short cloaks
and carrying little cudgels as Spartans did. Aristophanes even
coined a Greek word for them. He called them *esokritoun*—
"Socratified."

Did that get Socrates into trouble?

For a long time no one took these young men seriously;
their infatuation with Sparta and Socrates was a joke. But then
the joke suddenly went sour.

What do you mean?

The joke became what we would call, in Justice Holmes's
famous phrase, a "clear and present danger." In the last decade

and a half of the life of Socrates, these young aristocrats—in the wake of Athenian military defeats and with the connivance of the Spartans—twice overthrew the democracy and became the bully boys, the hit squads and storm troopers of rapacious dictatorships. Life, liberty, and property were never as insecure in Athens as under these two anti-democratic regimes. The first overthrow was in 411 B.C. The second, in 404 B.C., was led by Critias and Charmides, relatives of Plato and former students of Socrates. They appear as honored figures in the Platonic dialogues. This rebellious fringe of Athenian society made a third but unsuccessful attempt to overthrow the democracy again in 402 B.C., just three years before the trial of Socrates.

These three events shattered the confidence of the Athenians and made them less tolerant. But for this, Socrates would never have been brought to trial.

Are there trustworthy sources for all this?

The terror imposed on Athens by the rule of the so-called Four Hundred in 411 B.C. is told by Thucydides with his Olympian objectivity. The horrors of The Thirty in 404 B.C. are related with equal objectivity by Xenophon (though he was then living as an exile in Sparta) and confirmed by Aristotle in his work on the *Constitution of Athens.* Xenophon's history, the *Hellenica,* is also our source for the renewed threat to democracy in 402 B.C. These events are all part of the story that Plato does not tell.

What did Socrates do during the reign of The Thirty?

There was a struggle against The Thirty, and Socrates might have made himself a hero of the resistance if he had spoken against their rule or fled the city to join the opposition. Instead he stood above the battle, neither supporting nor opposing the dictators.

But didn't Xenophon in his Memorabilia—*or* Memoirs of Socrates—*picture Socrates as at odds with Critias and The Thirty?*

True, but that opposition was minimal and private. Socrates refused to take part in the arrest of the wealthy resident alien, Leon of Salamis. Leon was only one of many such *metics* of his class whom the dictators executed without trial in order to seize their property; The Thirty used Leon's property to pay the expenses of the Spartan garrison, which had occupied Athens and kept them in power.

Wasn't that praiseworthy as civil disobedience?

Indeed it was. But Socrates would have fared better at his trial—indeed I believe he would never have been indicted—if he had done more. If he had warned Leon of the danger, if he had made a public protest, if he—the lifelong teacher of virtue—had denounced these immoral and illegal acts, and especially if he had left the city to join the opposition. But throughout the conflict, he stayed in the city.

Why do you emphasize the phrase "stayed in the city"?

Under the amnesty that followed the restoration of democracy, no one except the oligarchic rulers could be prosecuted for anything they had done or failed to do before and during the dictatorship. But we know from legal pleadings in the following generation that to have "stayed in the city" during the conflict was regarded as shameful and could be used to prejudice the jury.

You mentioned earlier that Socrates deliberately set out to turn the jury against him. Where is the proof of this?

The evidence is in Xenophon's *Apology*. Unlike Plato's *Apology*, Xenophon's is not a masterpiece and is therefore little read. It is sketchy and seems to have been written soon after the trial. But Xenophon's plain and hasty account tells us things that Plato prefers to veil.

What does Xenophon add to the story?

Xenophon says that everybody who wrote about the trial

was surprised at the tone Socrates took in his own defense and felt that it could only serve to provoke a conviction.

Does Xenophon agree?

He agrees that the way Socrates handled his defense was hardly calculated to obtain an acquittal. But he says this should not have occasioned surprise because Socrates wanted to die.

That's not the impression from reading Xenophon's Apology *in translation.*

That's because the reverence for Socrates is such that most English versions of Xenophon's *Apology* have mistranslated a key word in the Greek text and confused the reader.

What word is that?

The word is *megalegoria* and it appears no less than three time on the first page. Let us take the Loeb bilingual edition as our example. There—I suppose for euphony—we find three different renderings of this one word: (1) "the loftiness of his words," (2) "his lofty utterance," and (3) "the sublimity of his speech."

What's wrong with that?

A sharp-eyed reader, even without the Greek text, will sense that something is wrong with these translations because Xenophon argues that "this was appropriate to the resolve he had made." The resolve was that Socrates had decided it was better to die than to be acquitted, since at seventy he believed that old age and its ailments would soon overtake him.

Isn't that quite plausible?

Indeed it is, and it also fits with Socrates' attitude as described by Plato. But what is implausible is this: If he wanted to die, why would he speak with loftiness or sublimity? Athenian juries were notoriously susceptible to elevated rhetoric and beauty of diction, as indeed they were to beauty in all its forms. To speak that way to the jurists would not have *antagonized* them. It would have swayed the jury to acquit. Socrates himself observes in Xenophon's account how often Athenian juries "have been carried away by an eloquent speech." So if *megalegoria* meant eloquence, it was hardly suited to what Xenophon says was Socrates' purpose.

So how do you solve that puzzle?

By taking a fresh look at the original text and the Greek language. And we find something fascinating: *megalegoria* did mean sublimity of expression at one time. But that meaning developed many centuries *after* the trial of Socrates, in writings on Greek rhetoric under the Roman Empire. At the time of the trial, *megalegoria*—literally "big talking"—meant boastfulness and arrogance of expression. This meaning is attested to by its usage in other works by Xenophon and those of other writers of the time. So you see, Xenophon is saying that Socrates was being arrogant and boastful. And that was well calculated to achieve what Socrates wanted—conviction and the death sentence.

Does Plato's account rebut Xenophon's?

On the contrary, if you reread the *Apology,* the *Crito,* and the *Phaedo* after reading Xenophon, you will see that Plato's version, though more subtle, dovetails with Xenophon's.

Give us an example.

What most antagonized the jury, as reported in both Plato and Xenophon, was Socrates' claim that the oracle at Delphi had termed him the wisest of men, as Xenophon puts it, or as Plato more enigmatically treats it, that no one was wiser than Socrates. In his *Apology,* Plato says that there was a *thorubos,* an angry outcry from the jury, when Socrates said this. Socrates felt it necessary to deny that he was boasting. In that denial Socrates uses the Greek expression *mega legein*—big talk or boasting. That is an exact synonym for the *megalegoria* in Xenophon.

Is there evidence elsewhere in Plato to support Xenophon?

Yes. In the *Crito,* after the trial, Socrates' disciples complain that he mishandled his defense. Later in the *Phaedo* they even suggest that he seems to have been bent on a kind of suicide.

How does Socrates answer that charge?

By an implicit admission. Socrates responds with a lovely but essentially nonsensical mystical discourse in which he argues that the philosopher should seek death as fulfillment because only in death is the soul freed from the body and able at last to contemplate the eternal and unchangeable Ideas. The *Phaedo* becomes a paean to death. It is a beautiful dialogue. But it certainly does not deny that in a sense Socrates gave himself the hemlock.

But are you not skipping ahead in the trial?

True. An Athenian trial had two phases. First the jury had to vote on whether to convict or not, and then on the penalty. Under Athenian procedure, the prosecution proposed one penalty and the defense another. The jury could not "split the difference": it had to vote one or the other. The prosecution proposed the death penalty. Then Socrates went on to antagonize the jury again by proposing counter-penalties the jury could hardly take seriously.

Are you relying now on Xenophon's account or Plato's?

Plato's is the fuller. He tells us how, in this concluding part of the trial, Socrates provoked the jury by a suggestion it was bound to consider offensive.

What was that?

In Athens, civic heroes and other distinguished persons were honored with free meals at the city hall. Socrates suggested that as his penalty he be given free meals there for the rest of his life. When this created an uproar of disapproval, he proposed a trivial fine. Only at last and too late, after appeals from Plato and other disciples that they were ready to put up the money, did he offer to pay a substantial fine. But by then the jury was too furious: it voted for the death penalty. It is worth knowing that the vote for the death penalty was much larger than the original vote for conviction. Many who had been ready to acquit now voted for death. *Megalegoria* had achieved its purpose.

How do you think Socrates should have handled his defense? What would you have advised if you had been his lawyer?

Actually Athens did not have lawyers in our sense. Litigants could hire speechwriters; Demosthenes was the most famous of them. Socrates didn't need one. He was the cleverest arguer in town and quite capable of a successful defense if he had wanted one.

Still, how would you have liked Socrates to handle his case?

I believe Socrates was unjustly accused, that no overt acts against the city were even alleged much less proven, that this was purely a prosecution for opinion—for what he had said and taught in the last few years of his life. As such it violated the city's most precious principles. Free speech was the very basis of its democracy, of the debates in the assembly where the laws were made, and in the jury courts in which those laws were interpreted. Free speech made possible the masterpieces, tragic and comic, of the Athenian theater—still among the wonders of world literature. I think that Socrates could have swung that narrow six-percent margin for conviction to acquittal if he had argued a free-speech defense.

But what makes you think that Athenians were conscious of free speech as a basic principle of government?

If a society is conscious of an idea, it will have a word for it. The Romans had no free speech in our sense and they had no word for it. But I found that the ancient Greeks had no less than four terms for free speech. That is more than in any other language.

What were those four words?

The oldest, first encountered in Aeschylus, is compounded

from the words for free, *eleutheros,* and mouth, *stomos.* The second turns up first in Herodotus, who made his history a prose epic in celebration of democracy, an account of the struggle of Greek democracy—especially Athenian—against Persian despotism. That word is *isegoria,* which etymologically means an equal right to speak in the assembly. It thus became a synonym for political equality.

What were the other two?

The next was *parrhasia,* a word believed to be of specific Athenian coinage. Its earliest appearance, as far as we can tell, is in the plays of Euripides. It referred to both that frankness on which the Athenians prided themselves and their right to free speech as citizens of a free city. It was a flag-waver of a word for Athenian audiences. Milton used a passage from Euripides at the very beginning of his *Areopagitica,* the noblest defense of a free press in modern times. How effectively Socrates might have used lines from Euripides to sway his jury for acquittal!

And what was the fourth?

Isologia, which means an equal right to speak. It appears in the history written by Polybius and has a special meaning for Americans. Polybius was the historian of the Achaean League, the first successful federal government in history, and the Framers of our Constitution looked to Polybius for inspiration in establishing our own federal system. Polybius attributes the stability and survival of this Greek federation—long after Greek freedom had been crushed elsewhere by Macedonian and Roman armies—to the fact that an equal right to speak, *isologia,* existed within the member cities and in their federal assembly or congress.

So how, specifically, if Socrates had wanted an acquittal, should he have argued his case?

If I had been his speechwriter, I would have had him say this:

"Men of Athens, fellow citizens, this is not a trial of Socrates but of ideas, and therefore of Athens. You are not prosecuting me for any unlawful or impious act against our city or its altars. No such evidence has been brought against me.

"You are not prosecuting me for anything I did, but for what I have said and taught. You are threatening me with death because you do not like my views and my teaching. This is a prosecution of ideas and that is something new in our city's history. In this sense, Athens is in the dock, not Socrates. Each of you, as my judges, is a defendant.

"Let me be frank. I do not believe in your so-called freedom of speech, but you do. I believe the opinions of ordinary men are only *doxa*—beliefs without substance; pale shadows of reality, not to be taken seriously, and likely only to lead a city astray.

"I think it absurd to encourage the free utterance of unfounded or irrational opinions, or to base civic policy on a count of heads, like cabbages. Hence I do not believe in democracy. But you do. This is your test, not mine.

"Your freedom of speech is based on the assumption that every man's opinion is of value, and that the many are better guides than the few. But how can you boast of your free speech if you suppress mine? How can you listen to the shoemaker's or the tanner's views when you debate justice in the assembly, but shut me up when I express mine?

"You are proud that the gates of Athens have been opened to philosophers from all over Greece and even the outer barbarian world. Will you now execute one of your own because suddenly you cannot stand to hear an unpopular opinion? It is not I but you who will be disgraced forever by my condemnation.

"You say my ideas have been corrupting the youth and leading them to question the democracy. You say that I was Critias's teacher. You are acting as if you had become his pupils.

"The Thirty were arbitrary, and did as they pleased. You

claim to be men who live by the law. Are you not acting like them? Tell me, now, by what law of Athens do you seek to restrict philosophic teaching? Where can I find it among the city's statutes? When was it debated and voted? Who proposed such a monstrosity, as you yourselves—in calmer days and in your right minds—would have termed it?

"The test of truly free speech is not whether what is said or taught conforms to any rule or ruler, few or many. Even under the worst dictator, it is not forbidden to agree with him. It is the freedom to disagree that constitutes freedom of speech. This has been the Athenian rule until now, the pride of our city, the glory on which your orators dwell. Will you turn your backs on it now?

"You say I have shown disrespect for the city's gods. Beware lest you make yourselves guilty of that very offense in condemning me. How can you honor Peitho—our civic goddess of persuasion—when persuasion is inhibited, and nonconformist thoughts prosecuted? Are you not disobeying Zeus Agoraios, the patron deity of free debate in the assembly, when you restrict debate by condemning me?

"Ideas are not as fragile as men. They cannot be made to drink hemlock. My ideas—and my example—will survive me. But the good name of Athens will wear a stain forever if you violate its traditions by convicting me. The shame will be yours, not mine."

You would have challenged them with a compliment?

Right. Had Socrates invoked freedom of speech as a basic right *of all Athenians,* he would have struck a deep and responsive chord. And I believe that the jury would have set him free.

Amy Tan

MOTHER TONGUE
1989

After earning a master's degree in linguistics from San Jose State
University, Amy Tan worked as a consultant for programs for disabled
children and then became a freelance writer. Her first book was the best-
selling novel *The Joy Luck Club,* which was a finalist for the National
Book Award in 1990 and was subsequently made into a film and play of
the same title. Her second novel, *The Kitchen God's Wife* (1991), was an
equally popular story of Chinese-American family life and an intense
mother-daughter relationship. Her essays have appeared in *The
Threepenny Review* and *Life;* her short stories have been published in
Atlantic Monthly, Grand Street, McCall's, and other magazines. Tan has
also written two children's books, *The Moon Lady* and *The Chinese
Siamese Cat.* Her novels have been translated into twenty-two languages.

I AM NOT A SCHOLAR OF ENGLISH or literature. I cannot give you much more than personal opinions on the
English language and its variations in this country or others.

I am a writer. And by that definition, I am someone who
has always loved language. I am fascinated by language in daily
life. I spend a great deal of my time thinking about the power of
language—the way it can evoke an emotion, a visual image, a
complex idea, or a simple truth. Language is the tool of my
trade. And I use them all—all the Englishes I grew up with.

Recently, I was made keenly aware of the different Englishes
I do use. I was giving a talk to a large group of people, the same
talk I had already given to half a dozen other groups. The nature
of the talk was about my writing, my life, and my book, *The Joy
Luck Club*. The talk was going along well enough, until I

remembered one major difference that made the whole talk sound wrong. My mother was in the room. And it was perhaps the first time she had heard me give a lengthy speech—using the kind of English I have never used with her. I was saying things like, "The intersection of memory upon imagination" and "There is an aspect of my fiction that relates to thus-and-thus"—a speech filled with carefully wrought grammatical phrases, burdened, it suddenly seemed to me, with nominalized forms, past perfect tenses, conditional phrases—all the forms of standard English that I had learned in school and through books, the forms of English I did not use at home with my mother.

Just last week, I was walking down the street with my mother, and I again found myself conscious of the English I was using, the English I do use with her. We were talking about the price of new and used furniture and I heard myself saying this: "Not waste money that way." My husband was with us as well, and he didn't notice any switch in my English. And then I realized why. It's because over the twenty years we've been together I've often used that same kind of English with him, and sometimes he even uses it with me. It has become our language of intimacy, a different sort of English that relates to family talk, the language I grew up with.

So you'll have some idea of what this family talk I heard sounds like, I'll quote what my mother said during a recent conversation which I videotaped and then transcribed. During this conversation, my mother was talking about a political gangster in Shanghai who had the same last name as her family's, Du, and how the gangster in his early years wanted to be adopted by her family which was rich by comparison. Later, the gangster became more powerful, far richer than my mother's family, and one day showed up at my mother's wedding to pay his respects. Here's what she said in part:

"Du Yusong having business like fruit stand. Like off the street kind. He is Du like Du Zong—but not Tsung-ming Island people. The local people call putong, the river east side, he belong to that side local people. That man want to ask Du Zong father take him in like become own family. Du Zong father wasn't look down on him, but didn't take seriously, until that man big like become a mafia. Now important person, very hard to inviting him. Chinese way, came only to show respect, don't stay for dinner. Respect for making big celebration, he shows up. Mean gives lots of respect. Chinese custom. Chinese social life that way. If too important won't have to stay too long. He come to my wedding. I didn't see, I heard it. I gone to boys' side, they have YMCA dinner. Chinese age I was nineteen."

You should know that my mother's expressive command of English belies how much she actually understands. She reads the Forbes report, listens to *Wall Street Week,* converses daily with her stockbroker, reads all of Shirley MacLaine's books with ease—all kinds of things I can't begin to understand. Yet some of my friends tell me they understand 50 percent of what my mother says. Some say they understand 80 to 90 percent. Some say they understand none of it, as if she were speaking pure Chinese. But to me, my mother's English is perfectly clear, perfectly natural. It's my mother tongue. Her language, as I hear it, is vivid, direct, full of observation and imagery. That was the language that helped shape the way I saw things, expressed things, made sense of the world.

Lately, I've been giving more thought to the kind of English my mother speaks. Like others, I have described it to people as "broken" or "fractured" English. But I wince when I say that. It has always bothered me that I can think of no way to describe it other than "broken," as if it were damaged and needed to be fixed, as if it lacked a certain wholeness and soundness. I've heard other terms used, "limited English," for example. But they seem just as bad, as if everything is limited, including people's perception of the limited English speaker.

I know this for a fact, because when I was growing up, my mother's "limited" English limited *my* perception of her. I was ashamed of her English. I believed that her English reflected the quality of what she had to say. That is, because she expressed them imperfectly her thoughts were imperfect. And I had plenty of empirical evidence to support me: the fact that people in department stores, at banks, and at restaurants did not take her seriously, did not give her good service, pretended not to understand her, or even acted as if they did not hear her.

My mother has long realized the limitations of her English as well. When I was fifteen, she used to have me call people on the phone to pretend I was she. In this guise, I was forced to ask for information or even to complain and yell at people who had been rude to her. One time it was a call to her stockbroker in New York. She had cashed out her small portfolio and it just so happened we were going to go to New York the next week, our very first trip outside California. I had to get on the phone and say in an adolescent voice that was not very convincing, "This is Mrs. Tan."

And my mother was standing in the back whispering loudly, "Why he don't send me check, already two weeks late. So mad he lie to me, losing me money."

And then I said in perfect English, "Yes, I'm getting rather concerned. You had agreed to send the check two weeks ago, but it hasn't arrived."

Then she began to talk more loudly, "What he want, I come to New York tell him front of his boss, you cheating me?" And I was trying to calm her down, make her be quiet, while telling the stockbroker, "I can't tolerate any more excuses. If I don't receive the check immediately, I am going to have to speak to your manager when I'm in New York next week." And sure enough, the following week there we were in front of this astonished stockbroker, and I was sitting there red-faced and quiet, and my mother, the real Mrs. Tan, was shouting at his boss in her impeccable broken English.

We used a similar routine just five days ago, for a situation that was far less humorous. My mother had gone to the hospital for an appointment, to find out about a benign brain tumor a CAT scan had revealed a month ago. She said she had spoken very good English, her best English, no mistakes. Still, she said, the hospital did not apologize when they said they had lost the CAT scan and she had come for nothing. She said they did not seem to have any sympathy when she told them she was anxious to know the exact diagnosis since her husband and son had both died of brain tumors. She said they would not give her any more information until the next time and she would have to make another appointment for that. So she said she would not leave until the doctor called her daughter. She wouldn't budge. And when the doctor finally called her daughter, me, who spoke in perfect English—lo and behold—we had assurances the CAT scan would be found, promises that a conference call on Monday would be held, and apologies for any suffering my mother had gone through for a most regrettable mistake.

I think my mother's English almost had an effect on limiting my possibilities in life as well. Sociologists and linguists probably will tell you that a person's developing language skills are more influenced by peers. But I do think that the language spoken in the family, especially in immigrant families which are more insular, plays a large role in shaping the language of the child. And I believe that it affected my results on achievement tests, IQ tests, and the SAT. While my English skills were never judged as poor, compared to math, English could not be considered my strong suit. In grade school, I did moderately well, getting perhaps B's, sometimes B-pluses in English, and scoring perhaps in the sixtieth or seventieth percentile on achievement tests. But those scores were not good enough to override the opinion that my true abilities lay in math and science, because in those areas I achieved A's and scored in the ninetieth percentile or higher.

This was understandable. Math is precise; there is only one correct answer. Whereas, for me at least, the answers on English tests were always a judgment call, a matter of opinion and personal experience. Those tests were constructed around items like fill-in-the-blank sentence completion, such as "Even though Tom was ———, Mary thought he was ———." And the correct answer always seemed to be the most bland combinations of thoughts, for example, "Even though Tom was shy, Mary thought he was charming," with the grammatical structure "even though" limiting the correct answer to some sort of semantic opposites, so you wouldn't get answers like "Even though Tom was foolish, Mary thought he was ridiculous." Well, according to my mother, there were very few limitations as to what Tom could have been, and what Mary might have thought of him. So I never did well on tests like that.

The same was true with word analogies, pairs of words, in which you were supposed to find some sort of logical, semantic relationship—for example, "'sunset' is to 'nightfall' as ——— is to ———." And here, you would be presented with a list of four possible pairs, one of which showed the same kind of relationship: "red" is to "stoplight," "bus" is to "arrival," "chills" is to "fever," "yawn" is to "boring." Well, I could never think that way. I knew what the tests were asking, but I could not block out of my mind the images already created by the first pair, "sunset is to nightfall"—and I would see a burst of colors against a darkening sky, the moon rising, the lowering of a curtain of stars. And all the other pairs of words—red, bus, stoplight, boring—just threw up a mass of confusing images, making it impossible for me to sort out something as logical as saying: "A sunset precedes nightfall" is the same as "a chill precedes a fever." The only way I would have gotten that answer right would have been to imagine an associative situation, for example, my being disobedient and staying out past sunset, catching a chill at night, which turns into feverish pneumonia as punishment, which indeed did happen to me.

I have been thinking about all this lately, about my mother's English, about achievement tests. Because lately I've been asked, as a writer, why there are not more Asian-Americans represented in American literature. Why are there few Asian-Americans enrolled in creative writing programs? Why do so many Chinese students go into engineering? Well, these are broad sociological questions I can't begin to answer. But I have noticed in surveys—in fact, just last week—that Asian students, as a whole, always do significantly better on math achievement tests than in English. And this makes me think that there are other Asian-American students whose English spoken in the home might also be described as "broken" or "limited." And perhaps they also have teachers who are steering them away from writing and into math and science, which is what happened to me.

Fortunately, I happen to be rebellious in nature, and enjoy the challenge of disproving assumptions made about me. I became an English major my first year in college after being enrolled as pre-med. I started writing nonfiction as a freelancer the week after I was told by my former boss that writing was my worst skill and I should hone my talents toward account management.

But it wasn't until 1985 that I finally began to write fiction. And at first I wrote using what I thought to be wittily crafted sentences, sentences that would finally prove I had mastery over the English language. Here's an example from the first draft of a story that later made its way into *The Joy Luck Club,* but without this line: "That was my mental quandary in its nascent state." A terrible line, which I can barely pronounce.

Fortunately, for reasons I won't get into today, I later decided I should envision a reader for the stories I would write. And the reader I decided upon was my mother, because these were stories about mothers. So with this reader in mind—and in fact, she did read my early drafts—I began to write stories using all the Englishes I grew up with: the English I spoke to my mother, which for lack of a better term might be described as "simple"; the English she used with me, which for lack of a better term might be described as "broken"; my translation of her Chinese, which could certainly be described as "watered down"; and what I imaged to be her translation of her Chinese if she could speak in perfect English, her internal language, and for that I sought to preserve the essence, but not either an English or a Chinese structure. I wanted to capture what language ability tests can never reveal: her intent, her passion, her imagery, the rhythms of her speech and the nature of her thoughts.

Apart from what any critic had to say about my writing, I knew I had succeeded where it counted when my mother finished reading my book, and gave me her verdict: "So easy to read."

Lewis Thomas

BECOMING A DOCTOR
1992

A research pathologist, Lewis Thomas served for many years as the president and chancellor of Memorial Sloan–Kettering Cancer Center in New York City. Like the poet and pediatrician William Carlos Williams, he never felt a need to choose between his devotion to science and letters. Rather, the two were intertwined in a productive way. His book *The Lives of a Cell* (winner of the National Book Award) appeared in 1974, followed by his essay collections, *The Medusa and the Snail* (1979) and *Late Night Thoughts on Listening to Mahler's Ninth Symphony* (1984), and his memoir of his life as a doctor, *The Youngest Science* (1983). "Becoming a Doctor" is taken from his last book, *The Fragile Species* (1992).

D OCTORS, DRESSED UP in one professional costume or another, have been in busy practice since the earliest records of every culture on earth. It is hard to think of a more dependable or enduring occupation, harder still to imagine any future events leading to its extinction. Other trades—goldsmithing, embalming, cathedral architecture, hexing, even philosophy—have had their ups and down and times of vanishing, but doctoring has been with us since we stumbled into language and society, and will likely last forever, or for as long as we become ill and die, which is to say forever.

What is it that we expected from our shamans, millennia ago, and still require from the contemporary masters of the profession? To *do* something, that's what.

The earliest sensation at the onset of illness, often preceding the recognition of identifiable symptoms, is apprehension.

Something has gone wrong, and a glimpse of mortality shifts somewhere deep in the mind. It is the most ancient of our fears. Something must be done, and quickly. Come, please, and help, or go, please, and find help. Hence, the profession of medicine.

You might expect that such a calling, with origins in deepest antiquity, would by this time have at hand an immense store of traditional dogma, volumes and volumes of it, filled with piece after piece of old wisdom, tested through the ages. It is not so. Volumes do exist, of course, but all of them are shiny new, and nearly all the usable knowledge came in a few months ago. Medical information does not, it seems, build on itself; it simply replaces structures already set in place, like the New York skyline. Medical knowledge and technical savvy are biodegradable. The sort of medicine that was practiced in Boston or New York or Atlanta fifty years ago would be as strange to a medical student or interne today as the ceremonial dance of a !Kung San tribe would seem to a rock festival audience in Hackensack.

I take it further. The dilemma of modern medicine, and the underlying central flaw in medical education and, most of all, in the training of internes, is this irresistible drive to do something, anything. It is expected by patients and too often agreed to by their doctors, in the face of ignorance. And, truth to tell, ignorance abounds side by side with the neat blocks of precise scientific knowledge brought into medicine in recent years.

It is no new thing. In 1876, on the occasion of the country's first centennial, a book entitled *A Century of American Medicine, 1776–1876,* was published. The five authors were indisputable authorities in their several fields, from the faculties of Harvard, Columbia, and Jefferson Medical College. The book is a summary of the major achievements in American medicine of the previous century. The optimistic last sentence in the book is perhaps more telling than the writers may have realized: "It is better to have a future than a past." A very large part of the past in that century of medicine was grim.

Early on, there was no such thing as therapeutic science, and beyond the efforts by a few physicians to classify human diseases and record the natural history of clinical phenomena, no sort of reliable empirical experience beyond anecdotes. Therapeutics was a matter of trial and error, with the trials based on guesswork and the guesses based mostly on a curious dogma inherited down the preceding centuries from Galen. Galen himself (c. 130–c. 200) had guessed wildly, and wrongly, in no less than five hundred treatises on medicine and philosophy, that everything about human disease could be explained by the misdistribution of "humors" in the body. Congestion of the various organs was the trouble to be treated, according to Galen, and by the eighteenth century the notion had been elevated to a routine cure-all, or anyway treat-all: remove the excess fluid, one way or another. The ways were direct and forthright: open a vein and take away a pint or more of blood at a sitting, enough to produce faintness and a bluish pallor, place suction cups on the skin to draw out lymph, administer huge doses of mercury or various plant extracts to cause purging, and if all else failed induce vomiting. George Washington perhaps died of this therapy at the age of sixty-six. Hale and hearty, he had gone for a horseback ride in the snow, later in the day had a fever and a severe sore throat, took to his bed, and called in his doctors. His throat was wrapped in poultices, he was given warm vinegar and honey to gargle, and over the next two days he was bled from a vein for about five pints of blood. His last words to his physician were, "Pray take no more trouble about me. Let me go quietly."

Beginning around the 1830s, medicine looked at itself critically, and began to change. Groups of doctors in Boston, Paris, and Edinburgh raised new questions, regarded as heretical by most of their colleagues, concerning the real efficacy of the standard treatments of the day. Gradually, the first example of science applied to clinical practice came somewhat informally into existence. Patients with typhoid fever and delirium tremens, two of the most uniformly fatal illnesses of the time, were divided into two groups. One was treated by bleeding, cupping, purging, and the other athletic feats of therapy, while the other group received nothing more than bed rest, nutrition, and observation. The results were unequivocal and appalling, and by the mid-nineteenth century medical treatment began to fall out of fashion and the era known as "therapeutic nihilism" was well launched.

The great illumination from this, the first revolution in medical practice in centuries, was the news that there were many diseases that are essentially self-limited. They would run their predictable course, if left to run that course without meddling, and, once run, they would come to an end and certain patients would recover by themselves. Typhoid fever, for example, although an extremely dangerous and potentially fatal illness, would last for five or six weeks of fever and debilitation, but at the end about 70 percent of the patients would get well again. Lobar pneumonia would run for ten to fourteen days and then, in lucky, previously healthy patients, the famous "crisis" would take place and the patients would recover overnight. Patients with the frightening manifestations of delirium tremens only needed to be confined to a dark room for a few days, and then were ready to come out into the world and drink again. Some were doomed at the outset, of course, but not all. The new lesson was that treating them made the outcome worse rather than better.

It is difficult to imagine, from this distance, how overwhelming this news was to most physicians. The traditional certainty had been that every disease was aimed toward a fatal termination, and without a doctor and his energetic ministrations, or barring miraculous intervention by a higher force, all sick people would die of their disease. To recognize that this was not so, and that with rare exceptions (rabies the most notable one) many sick people could get well by themselves, went against the accepted belief of the time. It took courage and determination, and time, to shake off the old idea.

Looking back over the whole embarrassing record, the historians of that period must be hard put to it for explanations of the steadily increasing demand, decade after decade, for more doctors, more clinics and hospitals, more health care. You might think that people would have turned away from the medical profession, or abandoned it. Especially since, throughout the last half of the nineteenth century and the full first third of this one, there was so conspicuously little that medicine had to offer in the way of effective drugs or indeed any kind of technology. Opium, digitalis, quinine, and bromides (for the "nerves") were the mainstays. What else did physicians do during all those years that kept their patients calling and coming?

Well, they did a lot of nontechnology, and it was immensely effective. Mainly, they made diagnoses, explained matters to the patient and family, and then stood by, taking responsibility. To be sure, there were skeptics and critics all around, but they had always been around. Montaigne wrote bluntly, concerning doctors: "I have known many a good man among them, most worthy of affection. I do not attack them, but their art. It is only fear of pain and death, and a reckless search for cures, which blinds us. It is pure cowardice that makes us so gullible." Molière made delightful fun of doctors in his century. Dickens had some affection but no great respect for the doctors, most of them odd, bumbling eccentrics, who turned up as minor but essential characters in all his novels. Shaw was a scathing critic of medicine and its pretensions, clear into modern times.

But the public regard, and loyalty, somehow held. It is

exemplified by a memorial tablet in the north wall of St. James Church in Piccadilly, in honor of Sir Richard Bright (1789–1858), the discoverer of the kidney disease which still bears his name, and a not-atypical Harley Street practitioner during the period of transition from the try-anything to the just-observe schools of medicine. The plaque reads, in part,

Sacred to the memory of Sir Richard Bright, M.D. D.C.L.
Physician Extraordinary to the Queen

He Contributed to Medical Science Many Scientific Discoveries
And Works of Great Value
And Died While In the Full Practice of His Profession
After a Life of Warm Affection
Unsullied Purity
And Great Usefulness

This is what nineteenth-century people expected their doctors to be, and believed most of them were in real life. The expectation survives to this day, but the reality seems to have undergone a change, in the public mind anyway.

There are many very good physicians around, as gifted and sought after as Bright was in his time, unquestionably better equipped by far to deal with life-threatening illnesses, trained to a level of comprehension of disease mechanisms beyond any nineteenth-century imagination, but "warm affection" and "unsullied purity" have an anachronistic sound these days, and even "great usefulness" is open to public questioning. The modern doctor is literally surrounded by items of high technology capable of preventing or reversing most of the ailments that used to kill people in their youth and middle years—most spectacularly, the bacterial and viral infections chiefly responsible for the average life expectancy of less than forty-five years in Bright's day. But medicine's agenda still contains a long list of fatal or incapacitating diseases, mostly the chronic disabilities of older people, and there is still no technology for these, not even yet a clear understanding of their underlying mechanisms.

The unequivocal successes include miliary tuberculosis, tertiary syphilis of the brain and heart, poliomyelitis, the childhood contagions, septicemias, typhoid, rheumatic fever and valvular heart disease, and most of the other great infectious diseases, now largely under control or already conquered. This was the result of the second big transformation in medicine, starting about fifty years ago with the introduction of the sulfonamides, penicillin, and the other antibiotics, gifts straight from science. The revolution continues in full force, thanks to what is now called the "biological revolution," but it is still in its early stages. With new technologies of fantastic power, such as recombinant DNA and monoclonal antibodies, disease mechanisms that were blank mysteries, totally inaccessible just a few years back, are now at least open to direct scrutiny in detail. The prospects for comprehending the ways in which cancer works, as well as other illnesses on what is becoming a long list, are now matters of high confidence and excitement among the younger researchers within the universities and in industrial laboratories.

But the future is not yet in sight, and medicine is still stuck, for an unknowable period, with formidable problems beyond the reach of therapy or prevention. The technologies for making an accurate diagnosis have been spectacularly effective, and at the same time phenomenally complex and expensive. This new activity is beginning to consume so much of the time of the students and internes, and the resources of the hospitals in which they do their work, that there is less and less time for the patient. Instead of the long, leisurely ceremony of history-taking, and the equally long ritual of the complete physical examination, and then the long explanations of what has gone wrong

and a candid forecast of what may lie ahead, the sick person perceives the hospital as an enormous whirring machine, with all
the professionals—doctors, nurses, medical students, aides and
porters—out in the corridors at a dead run. Questionnaires, fed
into computers along with items analyzing the patient's financial
capacity to pay the bills, have replaced part of the history. Blood
samples off to the laboratory, the CAT scan, and Nuclear
Magnetic Resonance machines are relied upon as more dependable than the physical examination.

Everyone, even the visitors, seems pressed for time. There is
never enough time, the whole place is overworked to near col-
lapse, out of breath, bracing for the next irremediable catastro-
phe—the knife wounds in the emergency ward, the flat lines on
the electroencephalogram, the cardiac arrests, and always everywhere on every ward and in every room the dying. The Hippo-
cratic adage "Art is long, Life is short" is speeded up to a blur.

Everyone is too busy, urgently doing something else, and
there is no longer enough time for the old meditative, specula-
tive ward rounds or the amiable conversations at bedside. The
house staff, all of them—internes, residents, junior fellows in for
the year on NIH training fellowships—are careening through
the corridors on their way to the latest "code" (the euphemism
for the nearly dead or the newly dead, who too often turn out to
be, in the end, the same), or deciphering computer messages
from the diagnostic laboratories, or drawing blood and injecting
fluids, or admitting in a rush the newest patient. The professors
are elsewhere, trying to allocate their time between writing out
their research requests (someone has estimated that 30 percent
of a medical school faculty's waking hours must be spent com-
posing grant applications), doing or at least supervising the
research in their laboratories, seeing their own patients (the sus-
tenance of a contemporary clinical department has become significantly dependent on the income brought in by the faculty's

collective private practice), and worrying endlessly about tenure (and parking). About the only professionals who are always on the wards, watching out for the unforeseen, talking and listening to the patients' families, are the nurses, who somehow manage, magically, to hold the place together for all its tendency to drift toward shambles.

I have only two proposals, more like obsessive wishes for the future than a recipe for the present. My first hope is for removal of substantial parts of the curriculum in the first two years, making enough room for a few courses in medical ignorance, so that students can start out with a clear view of the things medicine does not know. My second hope is for more research into the mechanisms of that still-unsolved list of human diseases. The trouble with medicine today is that we simply do not know enough, we are still a largely ignorant profession, faced by an array of illnesses which we do not really understand, unable to do much beyond trying to make the right diagnosis, shoring things up whenever we can by one halfway technology or another (the transplantation of hearts, kidneys, livers, and lungs are the only measures available when we lack any comprehension of the events responsible for the prior destruction of such organs). A great deal of the time and energy expended in a modern hospital is taken up by efforts to put off endgame.

We will be obliged to go on this way and at steadily increasing expense, as far as I can see, until we are rid of disease—at least rid of the ailments which now dominate the roster and fill the clinics and hospitals. This is not asking for as much as it sounds. We will never be free of our minor, self-limited ills, nor should we be planning on postponing dying beyond the normal human span of living—the seventies and eighties for most of us, the nineties for the few more (or less) lucky among us. But there is a great deal we will be able to do as soon as we have learned what to do, both for curing and preventing. It can never be done by guessing, as the profession learned in earlier centuries. Nor can very much be changed by the trendy fashions in changed "life-styles," all the magazine articles to the contrary; dieting, jogging, and thinking different thoughts may make us feel better while we are in good health, but they will not change the incidence or outcome of most of our real calamities. We are obliged, like it or not, to rely on science for any hope of solving such biological puzzles as Alzheimer's disease, schizophrenia, cancer, coronary thrombosis, stroke, multiple sclerosis, diabetes, rheumatoid arthritis, cirrhosis, chronic nephritis, and now, topping the list, AIDS. When we have gained a clear comprehension, in detail, of what has gone wrong in each of these, medicine will be earning its keep, in spades.

HOW MR. DEWEY DECIMAL
SAVED MY LIFE
1992

Since the publication of her first books a decade ago—the novel *The Bean Trees* (1988) and *Homeland and Other Stories* (1989)—Barbara Kingsolver has been a popular fiction writer, a reputation enhanced by the bestseller *Pigs in Heaven* in 1993 and *The Poisonwood Bible* in 1998. Her travel essays, commentaries on modern American culture, and memoirs of growing up in Kentucky have appeared in the *New York Times* and other publications and were collected in *High Tide in Tucson* in 1995. "How Mr. Dewey Decimal Saved My Life" is from that book.

A LIBRARIAN NAMED Miss Truman Richey snatched me from the jaws of ruin, and it's too late now to thank her. I'm not the first person to notice that we rarely get around to thanking those who've helped us most. Salvation is such a heady thing the temptation is to dance gasping on the shore, shouting that we are alive, till our forgotten savior has long since gone under. Or else sit quietly, sideswiped and embarrassed, mumbling that we really did know pretty much how to swim. But now that I see the wreck that could have been, without Miss Richey, I'm of a fearsome mind to throw my arms around every living librarian who crosses my path, on behalf of the souls they never knew they saved.

I reached high school at the close of the sixties, in the Commonwealth of Kentucky, whose ranking on educational spending was I think around fifty-first, after Mississippi and whatever was below Mississippi. Recently Kentucky has drastically changed the way money is spent on its schools, but back then, the wealth of the county decreed the wealth of the school, and few coins fell far from the money trees that grew in Lexington. Our county, out where the bluegrass begins to turn brown, was just scraping by. Many a dedicated teacher served out earnest missions in our halls, but it was hard to spin silk purses out of a sow's ear budget. We didn't get anything fancy like Latin or Calculus. Apart from English, the only two courses of study that ran for four consecutive years, each one building upon the last, were segregated: Home Ec for girls and Shop for boys. And so I stand today, a woman who knows how to upholster, color-coordinate a table setting, and plan a traditional wedding—valuable skills I'm still waiting to put to good use in my life.

As far as I could see from the lofty vantage point of age sixteen, there was nothing required of me at Nicholas County High that was going to keep me off the streets; unfortunately we had no streets, either. We had lanes, roads, and rural free delivery routes, six in number, I think. We had two stoplights, which were set to burn green in all directions after 6 P.M., so as not, should the event of traffic arise, to slow anybody up.

What we *didn't* have included almost anything respectable teenagers might do in the way of entertainment. In fact, there was one thing for teenagers to do to entertain themselves, and it was done in the backs of Fords and Chevrolets. It wasn't upholstering skills that were brought to bear on those backseats, either. Though the wedding-planning skills did follow.

I found myself beginning a third year of high school in a state of unrest, certain I already knew what there was to know, academically speaking—all wised up and no place to go. Some of my peers used the strategy of rationing out the Science and Math classes between periods of suspension or childbirth, stretching their schooling over the allotted four years, and I envied their broader vision. I had gone right ahead and used the classes up, like a reckless hiker gobbling up all the rations on day one of a long march. Now I faced years of Study Hall, with brief interludes of Home Ec III and IV as the bright spots. I was developing a lean and hungry outlook.

We did have a school library, and a librarian who was surely paid inadequately to do the work she did. Yet there she was, every afternoon, presiding over the study hall, and she noticed me. For reasons I can't fathom, she discerned potential. I expect she saw my future, or at least the one I craved so hard it must have materialized in the air above me, connected to my head by little cartoon bubbles. If that's the future she saw, it was riding down the road on the back of a motorcycle, wearing a black leather jacket with "Violators" (that was the name of our county's motorcycle gang, and I'm not kidding) stitched in a solemn arc across the back.

There is no way on earth I really would have ended up a Violator Girlfriend—I could only dream of such a thrilling fate. But I was set hard upon wrecking my reputation in the limited ways available to skinny, unsought-after girls. They consisted mainly of cutting up in class, pretending to be surly, and making up shocking, entirely untrue stories about my home life. I wonder now that my parents continued to feed me. I clawed like a cat in a gunnysack against the doom I feared: staying home to reupholster my mother's couch one hundred thousand weekends in a row, until some tolerant myopic farm boy came along to rescue me from sewing-machine slavery.

Miss Richey had something else in mind. She took me by the arm in study hall one day and said, "Barbara, I'm going to teach you Dewey Decimal."

One more valuable skill in my life.

She launched me on the project of cataloging and shelving every one of the, probably, thousand books in the Nicholas County High School library. And since it beat Home Ec III by a mile, I spent my study-hall hours this way without audible complaint, so long as I could look plenty surly while I did it. Though it was hard to see the real point of organizing books nobody ever looked at. And since it was my God-given duty in those days to be frank as a plank, I said as much to Miss Richey.

She just smiled. She with her hidden agenda. And gradually, in the process of handling every book in the room, I made some discoveries. I found *Gone With the Wind,* which I suspected my mother felt was kind of trashy, and I found Edgar Allan Poe, who scared me witless. I found that the call number for books about snakes is 666. I found William Saroyan's *Human Comedy,* down there on the shelf between Human Anatomy and Human Physiology, where probably no one had touched it since 1943. But I read it, and it spoke to me. In spite of myself I imagined the life of an immigrant son who believed human kindness was a tangible and glorious thing. I began to think about words like *tangible* and *glorious.* I read on. After I'd read all the good ones, I went back and read Human Anatomy and Human Physiology and found that I liked those pretty well too.

It came to pass in two short years that the walls of my high school dropped down, and I caught the scent of a world. I started to dream up intoxicating lives for myself that I could not have conceived without the books. So I didn't end up on a motorcycle. I ended up roaring hell-for-leather down the backroads of transcendent, reeling sentences. A writer. Imagine that.

The most important thing about the books I read in my rebellion is that they were not what I expected. I can't say I had no previous experience with literature; I grew up in a house full of books. Also, I'd known my way around the town's small library since I was tall enough to reach the shelves (though the town librarian disliked children and censored us fiercely) and looked forward to the Bookmobile as hungrily as more urbane children listened for the ice cream truck. So dearly did my parents want their children to love books they made reading aloud the center of our family life, and when the TV broke they took about two decades to get around to fixing it.

It's well known, though, that when humans reach a certain age, they identify precisely what it is their parents want for them and bolt in the opposite direction like lemmings for the cliff. I had already explained to my classmates, in an effort to get dates, that I was raised by wolves, and I really had to move on from there. If I was going to find a path to adult reading, I had to do it my own way. I had to read things I imagined my parents didn't want me looking into. Trash, like *Gone With the Wind.* (I think, now, that my mother had no real problem with *Gone With the Wind,* but wisely didn't let on.)

Now that I am a parent myself, I'm sympathetic to the longing for some control over what children read, or watch, or do. Our protectiveness is a deeply loving and deeply misguided effort to keep our kids inside the bounds of what we know is safe and right. Sure, I want to train my child to goodness. But unless I can invoke amnesia to blot out my own past, I have to see it's impossible to keep her inside the world I came up in. That world rolls on, and you can't step in the same river twice. The things that prepared me for life are not the same things that will move my own child into adulthood.

What snapped me out of my surly adolescence and moved me on were books that let me live other people's lives. I got to visit the Dust Bowl and London and the Civil War and Rhodesia. The fact that Rhett Butler said "damn" was a snoozer to me—I hardly noticed the words that mothers worried about. I noticed words like *colour bar,* spelled "colour" the way Doris Lessing wrote it, and eventually I figured out it meant racism. It was the thing that had forced some of the kids in my county to go to a separate school—which wasn't even a school but a one-room CME church—and grow up without plumbing or the hope of owning a farm. When I picked up *Martha Quest,* a novel set in southern Africa, it jarred open a door that was right in front of me. I found I couldn't close it.

If there is danger in a book like *Martha Quest,* and the works of all other authors who've been banned at one time or another, the danger is generally that they will broaden our experience and blend us more deeply with our fellow humans. Sometimes this makes waves. It made some at my house. We had a few rocky years while I sorted out new information about the human comedy, the human tragedy, and the ways some people are held to the ground unfairly. I informed my parents that I had invented a new notion called justice. Eventually, I learned to tone down my act a little. Miraculously, there were no homicides in the meantime.

Now, with my adolescence behind me and my daughter's still ahead, I am nearly speechless with gratitude for the endurance and goodwill of librarians in an era that discourages reading in almost incomprehensible ways. We've created for ourselves a culture that undervalues education (compared with the rest of the industrialized world, to say the least), undervalues breadth of experience (compared with our potential), downright discourages critical thinking (judging from what the majority of us watch and read), and distrusts foreign ideas. "Un-American," from what I hear, is meant to be an insult.

Most alarming, to my mind, is that we the people tolerate censorship in school libraries for the most bizarre and frivolous of reasons. Art books that contain (horrors!) nude human beings, and *The Wizard of Oz* because it has witches in it. Not always, everywhere, but everywhere, always something. And censorship of certain ideas in some quarters is enough to sway curriculums at the national level. Sometimes profoundly. Find a publishing house that's brave enough to include a thorough discussion of the principles of evolution in a high school text.

Good luck. And yet, just about all working botanists, zoologists, and ecologists will tell you that evolution is to their field what germ theory is to medicine. We expect our kids to salvage a damaged earth, but in deference to the religious beliefs of a handful, we allow an entire generation of future scientists to germinate and grow in a vacuum.

The parents who believe in Special Creation have every right to tell their children how the world was made all at once, of a piece, in the year 4004 B.C. Heaven knows, I tell my daughter things about economic justice that are just about as far outside the mainstream of American dogma. But I don't expect her school to forgo teaching Western history or capitalist economics on my account. Likewise, it should be the job of Special Creationist parents to make their story convincing to their children, set against the school's bright scenery of dinosaur fossils and genetic puzzle-solving, the crystal clarity of Darwinian logic, the whole glorious science of an evolving world that tells its own creation story. It cannot be any teacher's duty to tiptoe around religion, hiding objects that might raise questions at home. Faith, by definition, is impervious to fact. A belief that can be changed by new information was probably a scientific one, not a religious one, and science derives its value from its openness to revision.

If there is a fatal notion on this earth, it's the notion that wider horizons will be fatal. Difficult, troublesome, scary—yes, all that. But the wounds, for a sturdy child, will not be mortal. When I read Doris Lessing at seventeen, I was shocked to wake up from my placid color-blind coma into the racially segregated town I called my home. I saw I had been a fatuous participant in a horrible thing. I bit my nails to the quick, cast nets of rage over all I loved for a time, and quaked to think of all I had—still have—to learn. But if I hadn't made that reckoning, I would have lived a smaller, meaner life.

The crossing is worth the storm. Ask my parents. Twenty years ago I expect they'd have said, "Here, take this child, we will trade her to you for a sack of limas." But now they have a special shelf in their house for books that bear the family name on their spines. Slim rewards for a parent's thick volumes of patience, to be sure, but at least there are no motorcycles rusting in the carport.

My thanks to Doris Lessing and William Saroyan and Miss Truman Richey. And every other wise teacher who may ever save a surly soul like mine.

Ann S. Causey

IS HUNTING ETHICAL?
1992

As a student of botany and zoology and a former philosophy teacher at Auburn University in Alabama, Ann S. Causey is concerned with wildlife, ecology, and the nature of the questions we ask about both. "Is Hunting Ethical?" was originally written as a speech and was delivered to the first annual Governors' Symposium on North America's Hunting Heritage, held in Montana in 1992. The opening section (about the death of "Sandy") was added later when Causey reworked the speech into its present form as an essay. In the tradition of all serious philosophers, she is less interested in providing easy answers (and not at all willing to confirm preconceived opinions) than in examining the clarity of terms and rigor with which any fair debate is conducted.

~

THE STRUGGLING FAWN suddenly went limp in my arms. Panicked, I told my husband to pull the feeding tube out of her stomach. Though Sandy had quit breathing and her death was clearly imminent, I held her head down and slapped her back in an attempt to clear her trachea. Warm, soured milk ran from her mouth and nose, soaking my clothes and gagging us with its vile smell. I turned Sandy over in my arms, and my husband placed his mouth over her muzzle. While he blew air into her lungs, I squeezed her chest as a CPR course had taught me to do for human infants in cardiac arrest.

After a minute or so I felt her chest for a pulse. Nothing at first, then four weak beats in rapid succession. "She's alive! Keep breathing for her."

My husband gagged, then spit to avoid swallowing more of the soured milk, and continued his efforts to revive Sandy. I kept working her chest, hoping that through some miracle of will she would recover. Come on Sandy, wake up. Please wake up!

Sandy never woke up. My husband, a widlife biologist, and I had nursed over two dozen white-tailed deer fawns that summer for use in a deer nutrition and growth study he was conducting. Most of the animals were in poor shape when we got them. People around the state found them—some actually orphaned, others mistakenly thought to be abandoned. After a few days of round-the-clock feedings, the fun gave way to drudgery and frustration. That's when they would call their county conservation officer, who in turn called us.

All the animals we raised required and got from us loving care, attention, and patience, no matter how sick or recalcitrant they may have been. All were named, and we came to know each one as an individual with unique personality traits and behavior patterns. Though most lived to become healthy adults, each fatality was a tragic loss for us, and we mourned each and every death.

The afternoon Sandy died, however, was not convenient for mourning. We were going to a group dinner that evening and had to prepare a dish. Through tears I made a marinade for the roast. While the meat smoked over charcoal and hickory, we brooded over Sandy's death.

When the roast was done, we wiped away our tears, cleaned up, and went to the dinner. Our moods brightened as our roast was quickly gobbled up, and the evening's high point came when several guests declared that our roast was the best venison they'd ever eaten. The best deer meat. Part of an animal my husband, an avid hunter, had willfully killed and I had gratefully butchered, wrapped, and frozen—a deer that once was a cute and innocent little fawn . . . just like Sandy.

If any one word characterizes most people's feelings when

they reflect on the morality of killing an animal for sport, it is "ambivalence." With antihunters insisting that hunting is a demonstration of extreme irreverence for nonhuman life, thoughtful hunters must concede, albeit uncomfortably, the apparent contradiction of killing for sport while maintaining a reverence for life. Yet I know of few hunters who do not claim to have a deep reverence for nature and life, including especially the lives of the animals they seek to kill. It seems that this contradiction, inherent in hunting and increasingly the focus of debate, lies at the core of the moral conundrum of hunting. How can anyone both revere life and seek to extinguish it in pursuit of recreation? The opponents of hunting believe they have backed its proponents into a logical corner on this point, yet the proponents have far from given up the battle for logical supremacy. Is either side a clear winner?

None who know me or my lifestyle would label me "antihunting." Most of the meat in my diet is game. And many is the time I've defended hunting from the attacks of those who see all hunters as bloodthirsty, knuckle-dragging rednecks.

Yet I have on occasion found myself allied with antihunters. But it's an uneasy and selective alliance, my antihunting sentiments limited to diatribes against such blatantly unethical behavior as Big Buck contests, canned Coon Hunt for Christ rallies, and bumper stickers proclaiming "Happiness Is a Warm Gutpile."

There is also a subtler reason for my concerns about hunting, stemming, I believe from my disappointment with the responses of many hunters and wildlife managers to questions concerning the morality of hunting. In the interest of enlivening and, I hope, elevating the growing debate, it is these moral questions, and their answers, I wish to address here.

To begin, I should point out some errors, common to ethical reasoning and to the current debate, that we should do our best to avoid. The first is confusing prudence with morality. Pru-dence is acting with one's overall best interests in mind, while morality sometimes requires that one sacrifice self-interest in the service of a greater good.

While thorough knowledge is all that's required to make prudent decisions, the making of a moral decision involves something more: conscience. Obligations have no moral meaning without conscience. Ethical hunters do not mindlessly follow rules and lobby for regulations that serve their interests; rather, they follow their consciences, sometimes setting their own interests aside. In short, ethics are guided by conscience.

Another important distinction is between legality and morality. While many immoral activities are prohibited by law, not all behavior that is within the law can be considered ethical. The politician caught in a conflict of interest who claims moral innocence because he has broken no laws rarely convinces us. Nor should hunters assume that whatever the game laws allow or tradition supports is morally acceptable. The ethical hunter is obligated to evaluate laws and traditions in light of his or her own moral sense. Conscience is not created by decree or consensus, nor is morality determined by legality or tradition.

Finally, it's all too tempting to dismiss the concerns of our opponents by questioning their motives and credentials instead of giving serious consideration to the questions they raise. Hunters do hunting no favors by hurling taunts and slander at their opponents. The questions raised about hunting deserve a fair hearing on their own merits. Consideration of antihunting messages must not be biased by personal opinions of the messengers, nor should hunters' efforts remain focused on discrediting their accusers. Rather, ethical hunters must undertake the uncomfortable and sometimes painful processes of moral deliberation and personal and collective soul-searching that these questions call for.

•

The first difficulty we encounter in addressing the morality of hunting is identifying and understanding the relevant questions and answers. To me, the most striking feature of the current debate is the two sides' vastly different understanding of the meaning of the question, Is hunting a morally acceptable activity?

Those who support hunting usually respond by citing data. They enumerate the acres of habitat protected by hunting-generated funds; how many game species have experienced population increases due to modern game management; how much the economy is stimulated by hunting-related expenditures; how effectively modern game laws satisfy the consumptive and recreational interests of the hunting community today while assuring continued surpluses of game for future hunters; and how hunters, more than most citizens, care deeply about ecosystem integrity and balance and the global environment.

While these statements may be perfectly true, they're almost totally irrelevant to the question. Antihunters are not asking whether hunting is an effective management tool, whether it's economically advisable, or whether hunters love and appreciate nature. Rather, they're asking, Is it ethical to kill animals for sport? Are any forms of hunting morally right?

The hunter says yes; the antihunter says no, yet they are answering entirely different questions. The hunter answers, with data, what he or she perceives as a question about utility and prudence; the antihunter, though, has intended to ask a question about morality, about human responsibilities and values. It's as if one asked what day it is and the other responded by giving the time. While the answer may be correct, it's meaningless in the context of the question asked.

The point is that moral debates, including this one, are not about facts but about values. Moral controversy cannot be resolved by examination of data or by appeal to scientific studies.

An obsession with "sound, objective science" in addressing their opponents has led many hunters not only to avoid the crucial issues but to actually fuel the fires of the antihunting movement. Animal welfare proponents and the general public are primarily concerned about the pain, suffering, and loss of life inflicted on hunted animals, and the motives and attitudes of those who hunt. They're offended by references to wild animals as "resources." They're angered by the sterile language and, by implication, the emotionally sterile attitudes of those who speak of "culling," "controlling," "harvesting," and "managing" animals for "maximum sustained yield." And they're outraged by those who cite habitat protection and human satisfaction data while totally disregarding the interests of the sentient beings who occupy that habitat and who, primarily through their deaths, serve to satisfy human interests.

Antihunters insist that nontrivial reasons be given for intentional human-inflicted injuries and deaths—or that these injuries and deaths be stopped. An eminently reasonable request.

Even when hunters acknowledge the significance of the pain and suffering inflicted through hunting, they too often offer in defense that they feel an obligation to give back more than they take, and that hunters and wildlife professionals successfully have met this obligation. Granted, it may be that the overall benefits to humans and other species that accrue from hunting outweigh the costs to the hunted. Nevertheless, this utilitarian calculation fails to provide moral justification for hunting. Is it just, hunting's detractors ask, that wild animals should die to feed us? To clothe us? To decorate our bodies and den walls? To provide us with entertainment and sport?

These are the questions hunters are being asked. *These* are the questions they must carefully consider and thoughtfully address. It will not suffice to charge their opponents with biological naïveté, as theirs are not questions of science. Nor will charges of emotionalism quiet their accusers, since emotion plays an integral and valid part in value judgments and moral development. Both sides have members who are guided by their hearts, their minds, or both. Neither side has a monopoly on hypocrisy, zealotry, narrow-mindedness, or irrationalism. Opposition to hunting is based in largest part on legitimate philosophical differences.

It has been said that hunting is the most uncivilized and primitive activity in which a modern person can legally engage. Therein lies ammunition for the biggest guns in the antihunters' arsenal; paradoxically, therein also lies its appeal to hunters and the source of its approval by many sympathetic nonhunters.

Hunting is one of few activities that allows an individual to participate directly in the life and death cycles on which all natural systems depend. The skilled hunter's ecological knowledge is holistic and realistic; his or her awareness involves all the senses. Whereas ecologists study systems from without, examining and analyzing from a perspective necessarily distanced from their subjects, dedicated hunters live and learn from within, knowing parts of nature as only a parent or child can know his or her own family. One thing necessary for a truly ethical relationship with wildlife is an appreciation of ecosystems, of natural processes. Such an appreciation may best be gained through familiarity, through investment of time and effort, through curiosity, and through an attitude of humility and respect. These are the lessons that hunting teaches its best students.

Not only have ethical hunters resisted the creeping alienation between humans and the natural out-of-doors, they have fought to resist the growing alienation between humans and the "nature" each person carries within. Hunters celebrate their evolutionary heritage and stubbornly refuse to be stripped of their atavistic urges—they refuse to be sterilized by modern culture and thus finally separated from nature. The ethical hunter transcends the mundane, the ordinary, the predictable, the structured, the artificial. As Aldo Leopold argues in his seminal work *A Sand County Almanac,* hunting in most forms maintains a valuable element in the cultural heritage of all peoples.

Notice, though, that Leopold does not give a blanket stamp of moral approval to hunting; nor should we. In fact, Leopold recognized that some forms of hunting may be morally depleting. If we offer an ecological and evolutionary defense for hunting, as Leopold did and as many of hunting's supporters do today, we must still ask ourselves, For which forms of hunting is our defense valid?

The open-minded hunter should carefully consider the following questions: To what extent is shooting an animal over bait or out of a tree at close range after it was chased up there by a dog a morally enriching act? Can shooting an actually or functionally captive animal enhance one's understanding of natural processes? Does a safari to foreign lands to step out of a Land Rover and shoot exotic animals located for you by a guide honor your cultural heritage? Does killing an animal you profess to honor and respect, primarily in order to obtain a trophy, demonstrate reverence for the animal as a sentient creature? Is it morally enriching to use animals as mere objects, as game pieces in macho contests where the only goal is to outcompete other hunters? Is an animal properly honored in death by being reduced to points, inches, and pounds, or to a decoration on a wall? Which forms of hunting can consistently and coherently be defended as nontrivial, meaningful, ecologically sound, and morally enriching?

Likewise, we who hunt or support hunting must ask ourselves: Does ignoring, downplaying, and in some cases denying the wounding rate in hunting, rather than taking all available effective measures to lower it, demonstrate reverence for life? Does lobbying for continued hunting of species whose populations are threatened or of uncertain status exemplify ecological awareness and concern? Is the continued hunting of some declining waterfowl populations, the aerial killing of wolves in Alaska, or the setting of hunting seasons that in some areas may sentence to slow death the orphaned offspring of their legally killed lactating mothers, consistent with management *by* hunters—or do these things verify the antihunters' charges of management primarily *for* hunters?

These questions and others have aroused hunters' fears, indignation, defensive responses, and collective denial. Yet no proponent of ethical hunting has anything to fear from such questions. These are questions we should have been asking ourselves, and defensibly answering, all along. The real threat comes not from outside criticism but from our own complacency and uncritical acceptance of hunting's status quo, and from our mistaken belief that to protect *any* form of hunting, we must defend and protect *all* forms. In fact, to protect the privilege of morally responsible hunting, we must attack and abolish the unacceptable acts, policies, and attitudes within our ranks that threaten all hunting, as a gangrenous limb threatens the entire body.

The battle cry "Reverence for Life" has been used by both sides, at times with disturbing irony. Cleveland Amory, founder of the Fund for Animals, described in the June 1992 issue of *Sierra* magazine the perfect world he would create if he were appointed its ruler: "All animals will not only be not shot, they will be protected—not only from people but as much as possible from each other. Prey will be separated from predator, and there will be no overpopulation or starvation because all will be controlled by sterilization or implant."

A reverence for life? Only if you accept the atomistic and

utterly unecological concept of life as a characteristic of individuals rather than systems.

But neither can all who hunt legitimately claim to hold a reverence for life. In a hunting video titled "Down to Earth," a contemporary rock star and self-proclaimed "whack master" and "gutpile addict" exhorts his protégés to "whack 'em, stack 'em, and pack 'em." After showing a rapid sequence of various animals being hit by his arrows, the "master whacker" kneels and sarcastically asks for "a moment of silence" while the viewer is treated to close-up, slow-motion replays of the hits, including sickening footage of some animals that clearly are gut shot or otherwise sloppily wounded. A reverence for life? Such behavior would seem to demonstrate shocking *irreverence,* arrogance, and hubris. As hunters, we toe a fine line between profundity and profanity and must accept the responsibility of condemning those practices and attitudes that trivialize, shame, and desecrate all hunting. To inflict death without meaningful and significant purpose, to kill carelessly or casually, or to take a life without solemn gratitude is inconsistent with genuine reverence for life.

To be ethical, we must do two things: we must *act* ethically, and we must *think* ethically. The hunting community has responded to its critics by trying to clean up its visible act: we don't hear many public proclamations of gutpile addictions anymore; we less frequently see dead animals used as hood ornaments while the meat, not to be utilized anyway, rapidly spoils; those who wound more animals than they kill are less likely nowadays to brag about it; and, since studies show that the public opposes sport hunting as trivial, hunters are coached to avoid the term "sport" when they address the public or their critics.

What's needed, though, for truly ethical hunting to flourish is not just a change of appearance or vocabulary but a change of mind-set, a deepening of values. Hunters may be able to "beat" antihunters through a change of tactics, but to win the wrong war is no victory at all. Some morally repugnant forms of hunting are *rightfully* under attack, and we can defend them only by sacrificing our intellectual and moral integrity. We should do all we can to avoid such "victories." Hunters must reexamine and, when appropriate, give up some of what they now hold dear—not just because doing so is expedient but because it's *right.* As T. S. Eliot, quoted by Martin Luther King, Jr., in his "Letter from a Birmingham Jail," reminds us, "The last temptation is the greatest treason: To do the right deed for the wrong reason."

Can anyone give us a final answer to the question, Is hunting ethical?

No.

For one thing, the question and its answer depend heavily on how one defines "hunting." There are innumerable activities that go by this term, yet many are so different from one another that they scarcely qualify for the same appellation. Moreover, there is no one factor that motivates one hunter on each hunt; nor is there such a thing as the hunter's mind-set.

Second, and even more important, is the recognition that in most cases one cannot answer moral questions for others. Two morally mature people may ponder the same ethical dilemma and come to opposite, and equally valid, conclusions. The concept of ethical hunting is pluralistic, as hard to pin down as the definition of a virtuous person. Unlike our opponents, we who are hunting proponents do not seek to impose a particular lifestyle, morality, or spirituality on all citizens; we merely wish to preserve a variety of options and individualities in all our choices concerning responsible human recreation, engagement with nature, and our place in the food web. It's doubtful that any one system, whether it be "boutique" hunting, vegetarianism, or modern factory farming, is an adequate way to meet the ethical challenges of food procurement and human/nonhuman relationships in our diverse culture and burgeoning population.

Like education of any sort, moral learning cannot be passively acquired. In fact, the importance of answering the question of whether hunting is ethical is often exaggerated, for the value of ethics lies not so much in the product, the answers, as in the process of deep and serious deliberation of moral issues. To ponder the value of an animal's life versus a hunter's material and spiritual needs and to consider an animal's pain, suffering, and dignity in death is to acknowledge deeper values and to demonstrate more moral maturity than one who casually, defensively dismisses such ideas.

No matter the result, the process of moral deliberation is necessarily enriching. Neither side can offer one answer for all; we can only answer this question each for ourself, and even then we must be prepared to offer valid, consistent moral arguments in support of our conclusions. This calls for a level of soul-searching and critical thinking largely lacking on both sides of the current debate.

Today's ethical hunter must abandon the concept of hunting as fact and replace it with the more appropriate concept of hunting as challenge—the challenge of identifying and promoting those attitudes toward wildlife that exemplify the values on which morally responsible hunting behavior is based. Heel-digging and saber-rattling must give way to cooperation, to increased awareness and sensitivity, to reason and critical analysis, and to honest self-evaluation and assessment.

The Chinese have a wonderful term, *wei chi,* that combines two concepts: crisis . . . and opportunity. The term conveys the belief that every crisis presents an opportunity. I submit that the hunting community today faces its greatest crisis ever and, therein, its greatest opportunity—the opportunity for change, for moral growth, for progress.

THE FINE ART OF
BALONEY DETECTION
1995

For many years Carl Sagan was a professor of astronomy at Cornell University, though the titles of a few of his many books suggest his unusual range of interests: *A Path Where No Man Thought: Nuclear Winter and the End of the Arms Race* (with Richard Turco), *Shadows of Forgotten Ancestors: A Search for Who We Are* (with Ann Druyan), and *Pale Blue Dot: A Vision of the Human Future in Space.* A project of special importance to Sagan was narrowing the gap between specialists and the general public. His book *Cosmos,* published in conjunction with his Emmy Award–winning television series of the same title, sold more copies than any other English-language science book. A classic "popularizer" and a serious scholar, Sagan was the recipient of the Pulitzer Prize and NASA Medals for Exceptional Scientific Achievement and Distinguished Public Service.

M Y PARENTS DIED YEARS AGO. I was very close to them. I still miss them terribly. I know I always will. I long to believe that their essence, their personalities, what I loved so much about them, are—really and truly—still in existence somewhere. I wouldn't ask very much, just five or ten minutes a year, say, to tell them about their grandchildren, to catch them up on the latest news, to remind them that I love them. There's a part of me—no matter how childish it sounds—that wonders how they are. "Is everything all right?" I want to ask. The last words I found myself saying to my father, at the moment of his death, were "Take care."

Sometimes I dream that I'm talking to my parents, and suddenly—still immersed in the dreamwork—I'm seized by the overpowering realization that they didn't really die, that it's all been some kind of horrible mistake. Why, here they are, alive and well, my father making wry jokes, my mother earnestly advising me to wear a muffler because the weather is chilly. When I wake up I go through an abbreviated process of mourning all over again. Plainly, there's something within me that's ready to believe in life after death. And it's not the least bit interested in whether there's any sober evidence for it.

So I don't guffaw at the woman who visits her husband's grave and chats him up every now and then, maybe on the anniversary of his death. It's not hard to understand. And if I have difficulties with the ontological status of who she's talking to, that's all right. That's not what this is about. This is about humans being human. More than a third of American adults believe that on some level they've made contact with the dead. The number seems to have jumped by 15 percent between 1977 and 1988. A quarter of Americans believe in reincarnation.

But that doesn't mean I'd be willing to accept the pretensions of a "medium," who claims to channel the spirits of the dear departed, when I'm aware the practice is rife with fraud. I know how much I want to believe that my parents have just abandoned the husks of their bodies, like insects or snakes molting, and gone somewhere else. I understand that those very feelings might make me easy prey even for an unclever con, or for normal people unfamiliar with their unconscious minds, or for those suffering from a dissociative psychiatric disorder. Reluctantly, I rouse some reserves of skepticism.

How is it, I ask myself, that channelers never give us verifiable information otherwise unavailable? Why does Alexander the Great never tell us about the exact location of his tomb, Fermat about his Last Theorem, John Wilkes Booth about the Lincoln assassination conspiracy, Hermann Göring about the Reichstag fire? Why don't Sophocles, Democritus, and

Aristarchus dictate their lost books? Don't they wish future generations to have access to their masterpieces?

If some good evidence for life after death were announced, I'd be eager to examine it; but it would have to be real scientific data, not mere anecdote. As with the face on Mars and alien abductions, better the hard truth, I say, than the comforting fantasy. And in the final tolling it often turns out that the facts are more comforting than the fantasy.

The fundamental premise of "channeling," spiritualism, and other forms of necromancy is that when we die we don't. Not exactly. Some thinking, feeling, and remembering part of us continues. That whatever-it-is—a soul or spirit, neither matter nor energy, but something else—can, we are told, re-enter the bodies of human and other beings in the future, and so death loses much of its sting. What's more, we have an opportunity, if the spiritualist or channeling contentions are true, to make contact with loved ones who have died.

J. Z. Knight of the State of Washington claims to be in touch with a 35,000–year-old somebody called "Ramtha." He speaks English very well, using Knight's tongue, lips and vocal cords, producing what sounds to be an accent from the Indian Raj. Since most people know how to talk, and many—from children to professional actors—have a repertoire of voices at their command, the simplest hypothesis is that Ms. Knight makes "Ramtha" speak all by herself, and that she has no contact with disembodied entities from the Pleistocene Ice Age. If there's evidence to the contrary, I'd love to hear it. It would be considerably more impressive if Ramtha could speak by himself, without the assistance of Ms. Knight's mouth. Failing that, how might we test the claim? (The actress Shirley MacLaine attests that Ramtha was her brother in Atlantis, but that's another story.)

Suppose Ramtha were available for questioning. Could we

verify whether he is who he says he is? How does he know that he lived 35,000 years ago, even approximately? What calendar does he employ? Who is keeping track of the intervening millennia? Thirty-five thousand plus or minus what? What were things like 35,000 years ago? Either Ramtha really is 35,000 years old, in which case we discover something about that period, or he's a phony and he'll (or rather she'll) slip up.

Where did Ramtha live? (I know he speaks English with an Indian accent, but where 35,000 years ago did they do that?) What was the climate? What did Ramtha eat? (Archaeologists know something about what people ate back then.) What were the indigenous languages, and social structure? Who else did Ramtha live with—wife, wives, children, grandchildren? What was the life cycle, the infant mortality rate, the life expectancy? Did they have birth control? What clothes did they wear? How were the clothes manufactured? What were the most dangerous predators? Hunting and fishing implements and strategies? Weapons? Endemic sexism? Xenophobia and ethnocentrism? And if Ramtha came from the "high civilization" of Atlantis, where are the linguistic, technological, historical and other details? What was their writing like? Tell us. Instead, all we are offered are banal homilies.

Here, to take another example, is a set of information channeled not from an ancient dead person, but from unknown non-human entities who make crop circles, as recorded by the journalist Jim Schnabel:

We are so anxious at this sinful nation spreading lies about us. We do not come in machines, we do not land on your earth in machines . . . We come like the wind. We are Life Force. Life Force from the ground . . . Come here . . . We are but a breath away . . . a breath away . . . we are not a million miles away . . . a Life Force that is larger than the

energies in your body. But we meet at a higher level of life
. . . We need no name. We are parallel to your world,
alongside your world . . . The walls are broken. Two men
will rise from the past . . . the great bear . . . the world will
be at peace.

People pay attention to these puerile marvels mainly because
they promise something like old-time religion, but especially life
after death, even life eternal.

A very different prospect for something like eternal life was
once proposed by the versatile British scientist J. B. S. Haldane,
who was, among many other things, one of the founders of
population genetics. Haldane imagined a far future when the
stars have darkened and space is mainly filled with a cold, thin
gas. Nevertheless, if we wait long enough statistical fluctuations
in the density of this gas will occur. Over immense periods of
time the fluctuations will be sufficient to reconstitute a Universe
something like our own. If the Universe is infinitely old, there
will be an infinite number of such reconstitutions, Haldane
pointed out.

So in an infinitely old universe with an infinite number of
appearances of galaxies, stars, planets, and life, an identical
Earth must reappear on which you and all your loved ones will
be reunited. I'll be able to see my parents again and introduce
them to the grandchildren they never knew. And all this will
happen not once, but an infinite number of times.

Somehow, though, this does not quite offer the consolations
of religion. If none of us is to have any recollection of what happened *this* time around, the time the reader and I are sharing,
the satisfactions of bodily resurrection, in my ears at least, ring
hollow.

But in this reflection I have underestimated what infinity
means. In Haldane's picture, there will be universes, indeed an

infinite number of them, in which our brains will have full rec-ollection of many previous rounds. Satisfaction is at hand—tempered, though, by the thought of all those other universes which will also come into existence (again, not once but an infi-nite number of times) with tragedies and horrors vastly outstrip-ping anything I've experienced this turn.

The Consolation of Haldane depends, though, on what kind of universe we live in, and maybe on such arcana as whether there's enough matter to eventually reverse the expan-sion of the universe, and the character of vacuum fluctuations. Those with a deep longing for life after death might, it seems, devote themselves to cosmology, quantum gravity, elementary particle physics, and transfinite arithmetic.

Clement of Alexandria, a Father of the early Church, in his *Exhortations to the Greeks* (written around the year 190) dis-missed pagan beliefs in words that might today seem a little ironic:

> Far indeed are we from allowing grown men to listen to such tales. Even to our own children, when they are crying their heart out, as the saying goes, we are not in the habit of telling fabulous stories to soothe them.

In our time we have less severe standards. We tell children about Santa Claus, the Easter Bunny, and the Tooth Fairy for reasons we think emotionally sound, but then disabuse them of these myths before they're grown. Why retract? Because their well-being as adults depends on them knowing the world as it really is. We worry, and for good reason, about adults who still believe in Santa Claus.

On doctrinaire religions, "Men dare not avow, even to their own hearts," wrote the philosopher David Hume, the doubts which they entertain on such subjects. They make a merit of implicit faith; and disguise to themselves their real infidelity, by the strongest asseverations and the most positive bigotry.

This infidelity has profound moral consequences, as the American revolutionary Tom Paine wrote in *The Age of Reason:*

> Infidelity does not consist in believing, or in disbelieving; it consists in professing to believe what one does not believe. It is impossible to calculate the moral mischief, if I may so express it, that mental lying has produced in society. When man has so far corrupted and prostituted the chastity of his mind, as to subscribe his professional belief to things he does not believe, he has prepared himself for the commission of every other crime.

T. H. Huxley's formulation was

> The foundation of morality is to . . . give up pretending to believe that for which there is no evidence, and repeating unintelligible propositions about things beyond the possibilities of knowledge.

Clement, Hume, Paine, and Huxley were all talking about religion. But much of what they wrote has more general applications—for example to the pervasive background importunings of our commercial civilization: There is a class of aspirin commercials in which actors pretending to be doctors reveal the competing product to have only so much of the painkilling ingredient that doctors recommend most—they don't tell you what the mysterious ingredient is. Whereas *their* product has a dramatically larger amount (1.2 to 2 times more per tablet). So buy their product. But why not just take two of the competing tablets? Or consider the analgesic that works better than the "regular-strength" product of the competition. Why not then take the "extra-strength" competitive product? And of course they do not tell us of the more than a thousand deaths each year in the United States from the use of aspirin, or the roughly 5,000 annual cases of kidney failure from the use of acetaminophen, chiefly Tylenol. Or who cares which breakfast cereal has more vitamins when we can take a vitamin pill with breakfast? Likewise, why should it matter whether an antacid contains calcium if the calcium is for nutrition and irrelevant for gastritis? Commercial culture is full of similar misdirections and evasions at the expense of the consumer. You're not supposed to ask. Don't think. Buy.

Paid product endorsements, especially by real or purported experts, constitute a steady rainfall of deception. They betray contempt for the intelligence of their customers. They introduce an insidious corruption of popular attitudes about scientific objectivity. Today there are even commercials in which real scientists, some of considerable distinction, shill for corporations. They teach that scientists too will lie for money. As Tom Paine warned, inuring us to lies lays the groundwork for many other evils.

I have in front of me as I write the program of one of the annual Whole Life Expos, New Age expositions held in San Francisco. Typically, tens of thousands of people attend. Highly questionable experts tout highly questionable products. Here are some of the presentations: "How Trapped Blood Proteins Produce Pain and Suffering." "Crystals, Are They Talismans or Stones?" (I have an opinion myself.) It continues: "As a crystal focuses sound and light waves for radio and television"—this is a vapid misunderstanding of how radio and television work— "so may it amplify spiritual vibrations for the attuned human."

Or here's one: "Return of the Goddess, a Presentational Ritual." Another: "Synchronicity, the Recognition Experience." That one is given by "Brother Charles." Or, on the next page, "You, Saint-Germain, and Healing Through the Violet Flame." It goes on and on, with plenty of ads about "opportunities"—running the short gamut from the dubious to the spurious—that are available at the Whole Life Expo.

Distraught cancer victims make pilgrimages to the Philippines, where "psychic surgeons," having palmed bits of chicken liver or goat heart, pretend to reach into the patient's innards and withdraw the diseased tissue, which is then triumphantly displayed. Leaders of Western democracies regularly consult astrologers and mystics before making decisions of state. Under public pressure for results, police with an unsolved murder or a missing body on their hands consult ESP "experts" (who never guess better than expected by common sense, but the police, the ESPers say, keep calling). A clairvoyance gap with adversary nations is announced, and the Central Intelligence Agency, under Congressional prodding, spends tax money to find out whether submarines in the ocean depths can be located by thinking hard at them. A "psychic"—using pendulums over maps and dowsing rods in airplanes—purports to find new mineral deposits; an Australian mining company pays him top dollar up front, none of it returnable in the event of failure, and a share in the exploitation of ores in the event of success. Nothing is discovered. Statues of Jesus or murals of Mary are spotted with moisture, and thousands of kind-hearted people convince themselves that they have witnessed a miracle.

These are all cases of proved or presumptive baloney. A deception arises, sometimes innocently but collaboratively, sometimes with cynical premeditation. Usually the victim is caught up in a powerful emotion—wonder, fear, greed, grief. Credulous acceptance of baloney can cost you money; that's what P. T. Barnum meant when he said, "There's a sucker born every minute." But it can be much more dangerous than that, and when governments and societies lose the capacity for critical thinking, the results can be catastrophic—however sympathetic we may be to those who have bought the baloney.

In science we may start with experimental results, data, observations, measurements, "facts." We invent, if we can, a rich array of possible explanations and systematically confront each explanation with the facts. In the course of their training, scientists are equipped with a baloney detection kit. The kit is brought out as a matter of course whenever new ideas are offered for consideration. If the new idea survives examination by the tools in our kit, we grant it warm, although tentative, acceptance. If you're so inclined, if you don't want to buy baloney even when it's reassuring to do so, there are precautions that can be taken; there's a tried-and-true, consumer-tested method.

What's in the kit? Tools for skeptical thinking.

What skeptical thinking boils down to is the means to construct, and to understand, a reasoned argument and—especially important—to recognize a fallacious or fraudulent argument. The question is not whether we *like* the conclusion that emerges out of a train of reasoning, but whether the conclusion *follows* from the premise or starting point and whether that premise is true.

Among the tools:

• Wherever possible there must be independent confirmation of the "facts."

• Encourage substantive debate on the evidence by knowledgeable proponents of all points of view.

• Arguments from authority carry little weight—"authorities" have made mistakes in the past. They will do so again in the future. Perhaps a better way to say it is that in science there are no authorities; at most, there are experts.

• Spin more than one hypothesis. If there's something to be explained, think of all the different ways in which it *could* be explained. Then think of tests by which you might systematically disprove each of the alternatives. What survives, the hypothesis that resists disproof in this Darwinian selection among "multiple working hypotheses," has a much better chance of being the right answer than if you had simply run with the first idea that caught your fancy.[1]

• Try not to get overly attached to a hypothesis just because it's yours. It's only a way station in the pursuit of knowledge. Ask yourself why you like the idea. Compare it fairly with the alternatives. See if you can find reasons for rejecting it. If you don't, others will.

• Quantify. If whatever it is you're explaining has some measure, some numerical quantity attached to it, you'll be much better able to discriminate among competing hypotheses. What is vague and qualitative is open to many explanations. Of course there are truths to be sought in the many qualitative issues we are obliged to confront, but finding *them* is more challenging.

• If there's a chain of argument, *every* link in the chain must work (including the premise)—not just most of them.

• Occam's Razor. This convenient rule-of-thumb urges us when faced with two hypotheses that explain the data *equally well* to choose the simpler.

• Always ask whether the hypothesis can be, at least in principle, falsified. Propositions that are untestable, unfalsifiable are not worth much. Consider the grand idea that our Universe and everything in it is just an elementary particle—an electron, say—in a much bigger Cosmos. But if we can never acquire information from outside our Universe, is not the idea incapable of disproof? You must be able to check assertions out. Inveterate skeptics must be given the chance to follow your reasoning, to duplicate your experiments and see if they get the same result.

The reliance on carefully designed and controlled experiments is key, as I tried to stress earlier. We will not learn much from mere contemplation. It is tempting to rest content with the first candidate explanation we can think of. One is much better than none. But what happens if we can invent several? How do we decide among them? We don't. We let experiment do it. Francis Bacon provided the classic reason:

> Argumentation cannot suffice for the discovery of new work, since the subtlety of Nature is greater many times than the subtlety of argument.

Control experiments are essential. If, for example, a new medicine is alleged to cure a disease 20 percent of the time, we must make sure that a control population, taking a dummy sugar pill which as far as the subjects know might be the new drug, does not also experience spontaneous remission of the disease 20 percent of the time.

Variables must be separated. Suppose you're seasick, and given both an acupressure bracelet and 50 milligrams of meclizine. You find the unpleasantness vanishes. What did it—the bracelet or the pill? You can tell only if you take the one without the other, next time you're seasick. Now imagine that you're not so dedicated to science as to be willing to be seasick. Then you won't separate the variables. You'll take both remedies again. You've achieved the desired practical result; further knowledge, you might say, is not worth the discomfort of attaining it.

Often the experiment must be done "double-blind," so that those hoping for a certain finding are not in the potentially compromising position of evaluating the results. In testing a new medicine, for example, you might want the physicians who determine which patients' symptoms are relieved not to know which patients have been given the new drug. The knowledge might influence their decision, even if only unconsciously. Instead the list of those who experienced remission of symptoms can be compared with the list of those who got the new drug, each independently ascertained. Then you can determine what correlation exists. Or in conducting a police lineup or photo identification, the officer in charge should not know who the prime suspect is, so as not consciously or unconsciously to influence the witness.

In addition to teaching us what to do when evaluating a claim to knowledge, any good baloney detection kit must also teach us what *not* to do. It helps us recognize the most common and perilous fallacies of logic and rhetoric. Many good examples can be found in religion and politics, because their practitioners are so often obliged to justify two contradictory propositions. Among these fallacies are:

- *ad hominem*—Latin for "to the man," attacking the arguer and not the argument (e.g., *The Reverend Dr. Smith is a known Biblical fundamentalist, so her objections to evolution need not be taken seriously*);
- argument from authority (e.g., *President Richard Nixon should be re-elected because he has a secret plan to end the war in Southeast Asia*—but because it was secret, there was no way for the electorate to evaluate it on its merits; the argument amounted to trusting him because he was President: a mistake, as it turned out);
- argument from adverse consequences (e.g., *A God meting out punishment and reward must exist, because if He didn't, society*

would be much more lawless and dangerous—perhaps even ungovernable.[2] Or: *The defendant in a widely publicized murder trial must be found guilty; otherwise, it will be an encouragement for other men to murder their wives);*

• appeal to ignorance—the claim that whatever has not been proved false must be true, and vice versa (e.g., *There is no compelling evidence that UFOs are not visiting the Earth; therefore UFOs exist—and there is intelligent life elsewhere in the Universe.* Or: *There may be seventy kazillion other worlds, but not one is known to have the moral advancement of the Earth, so we're still central to the Universe.*) This impatience with ambiguity can be criticized in the phrase: absence of evidence is not evidence of absence.

• special pleading, often to rescue a proposition in deep rhetorical trouble (e.g., *How can a merciful God condemn future generations to torment because, against orders, one woman induced one man to eat an apple? Special plead: You don't understand the subtle Doctrine of Free Will.* Or: *How can there be an equally godlike Father, Son, and Holy Ghost in the same Person? Special plead: You don't understand the Divine Mystery of the Trinity.* Or: *How could God permit the followers of Judaism, Christianity, and Islam—each in their own way enjoined to heroic measures of loving kindness and compassion—to have perpetrated so much cruelty for so long? Special plead: You don't understand Free Will again. And anyway, God moves in mysterious ways.*)

• begging the question, also called assuming the answer (e.g., *We must institute the death penalty to discourage violent crime.* But does the violent crime rate in fact fall when the death penalty is imposed? Or: *The stock market fell yesterday because of a technical adjustment and profit-taking by investors*—but is there any *independent* evidence for the causal role of "adjustment" and profit-taking; have we learned anything at all from this purported explanation?);

• observational selection, also called the enumeration of favorable circumstances, or as the philosopher Francis Bacon described it, counting the hits and forgetting the misses[3] (e.g., *A state boasts of the Presidents it has produced, but is silent on its serial killers*);

• statistics of small numbers—a close relative of observational selection (e.g., *"They say 1 out of every 5 people is Chinese. How is this possible? I know hundreds of people, and none of them is Chinese. Yours truly."* Or: *"I've thrown three sevens in a row. Tonight I can't lose."*);

• misunderstanding of the nature of statistics (e.g., *President Dwight Eisenhower expressing astonishment and alarm on discovering that fully half of all Americans have below average intelligence*);

• inconsistency (e.g., *Prudently plan for the worst of which a potential military adversary is capable, but thriftily ignore scientific projections on environmental dangers because they're not "proved."* Or: *Attribute the declining life expectancy in the former Soviet Union to the failures of communism many years ago, but never attribute the high infant mortality rate in the United States (now highest of the major industrial nations) to the failures of capitalism.* Or: *Consider it reasonable for the Universe to continue to exist forever into the future, but judge absurd the possibility that it has infinite duration into the past*);

• *non sequitur*—Latin for "It doesn't follow" (e.g., *Our nation will prevail because God is great.* But nearly every nation pretends this to be true; the German formulation was *"Gott mit uns"*). Often those falling into the *non sequitur* fallacy have simply failed to recognize alternative possibilities;

• *post hoc, ergo propter hoc*—Latin for "It happened after, so it was caused by" (e.g., Jaime Cardinal Sin, Archbishop of Manila: *"I know of . . . a 26-year-old who looks 60 because she takes [contraceptive] pills."* Or: *Before women got the vote, there were no nuclear weapons*);

• meaningless question (e.g., *What happens when an irre-*

sistible force meets an immovable object? But if there is such a thing as an irresistible force there can be no immovable objects, and vice versa);

• excluded middle, or false dichotomy—considering only the two extremes in a continuum of intermediate possibilities (e.g., *"Sure, take his side; my husband's perfect; I'm always wrong."* Or: *"Either you love your country or you hate it."* Or: *"If you're not part of the solution, you're part of the problem"*);

• short-term vs. long-term—a subset of the excluded middle, but so important I've pulled it out for special attention (e.g., *We can't afford programs to feed malnourished children and educate pre-school kids. We need to urgently deal with crime on the streets.* Or: *Why explore space or pursue fundamental science when we have so huge a budget deficit?*);

• slippery slope, related to excluded middle (e.g., *If we allow abortion in the first weeks of pregnancy, it will be possible to prevent the killing of a full-term infant.* Or, conversely: *If the state prohibits abortion even in the ninth month, it will soon be telling us what to do with our bodies around the time of conception*);

• confusion of correlation and causation (e.g., *A survey shows that more college graduates are homosexual than those with lesser education; therefore education makes people gay.* Or: *Andean earthquakes are correlated with closest approaches of the planet Uranus; therefore—despite the absence of any such correlation for the nearer, more massive planet Jupiter—the latter causes the former* [4]);

• straw man—caricaturing a position to make it easier to attack (e.g., *Scientists suppose that living things simply fell together by chance*—a formulation that willfully ignores the central Darwinian insight, that Nature ratchets up by saving what works and discarding what doesn't. Or—this is also a short-term/long-term fallacy—*environmentalists care more for snail darters and spotted owls than they do for people*);

• suppressed evidence, or half-truths (e.g., *An amazingly*

accurate and widely quoted "prophecy" of the assassination attempt on President Reagan is shown on television; but—an important detail—was it recorded before or after the event? Or: *These government abuses demand revolution, even if you can't make an omelette without breaking some eggs.* Yes, but is this likely to be a revolution in which far more people are killed than under the previous regime? What does the experience of other revolutions suggest? Are all revolutions against oppressive regimes desirable and in the interests of the people?);

• weasel words (e.g., The separation of powers of the U.S. Constitution specifies that the United States may not conduct a war without a declaration by Congress. On the other hand, Presidents are given control of foreign policy and the conduct of wars, which are potentially powerful tools for getting themselves re-elected. Presidents of either political party may therefore be tempted to arrange wars while waving the flag and calling the wars something else—"police actions," "armed incursions," "protective reaction strikes," "pacification," "safeguarding American interests," and a wide variety of "operations," such as "Operation Just Cause." Euphemisms for war are one of a broad class of reinventions of language for political purposes. Talleyrand said, "An important art of politicians is to find new names for institutions which under old names have become odious to the public").

Knowing the existence of such logical and rhetorical fallacies rounds out our toolkit. Like all tools, the baloney detection kit can be misused, applied out of context, or even employed as a rote alternative to thinking. But applied judiciously, it can make all the difference in the world—not least in evaluating our own arguments before we present them to others.

The American tobacco industry grosses some $50 billion

per year. There is a statistical correlation between smoking and cancer, the tobacco industry admits, but not, they say, a causal relation. A logical fallacy, they imply, is being committed. What might this mean? Maybe people with hereditary propensities for cancer also have hereditary propensities to take addictive drugs—so cancer and smoking might be correlated, but the cancer would not be caused by the smoking. Increasingly farfetched connections of this sort can be contrived. This is exactly one of the reasons science insists on control experiments.

Suppose you paint the backs of large numbers of mice with cigarette tar, and also follow the health of large numbers of nearly identical mice that have not been painted. If the former get cancer and the latter do not, you can be pretty sure that the correlation is causal. Inhale tobacco smoke, and the chance of getting cancer goes up; don't inhale, and the rate stays at the background level. Likewise for emphysema, bronchitis, and cardiovascular diseases.

When the first work was published in the scientific literature in 1953 showing that the substances in cigarette smoke when painted on the backs of rodents produce malignancies, the response of the six major tobacco companies was to initiate a public relations campaign to impugn the research, sponsored by the Sloan–Kettering Foundation. This is similar to what the Du Pont Corporation did when the first research was published in 1974 showing that their Freon product attacks the protective ozone layer. There are many other examples.

You might think that before they denounce unwelcome research findings, major corporations would devote their considerable resources to checking out the safety of the products they propose to manufacture. And if they missed something, if independent scientists suggest a hazard, why would the companies protest? Would they rather kill people than lose profits? If, in an uncertain world, an error must be made, shouldn't it be biased toward protecting customers and the public? And, incidentally, what do these cases say about the ability of the free enterprise system to police itself? Aren't these instances where at least some government intrusion is in the public interest?

A 1971 internal report of the Brown and Williamson Tobacco Corporation lists as a corporate objective "to set aside in the minds of millions the false conviction that cigarette smoking causes lung cancer and other diseases; a conviction based on fanatical assumptions, fallacious rumors, unsupported claims and the unscientific statements and conjectures of publicity-seeking opportunists." They complain of

> the incredible, unprecedented and nefarious attack against the cigarette, constituting the greatest libel and slander ever perpetrated against any product in the history of free enterprise; a criminal libel of such major proportions and implications that one wonders how such a crusade of calumny can be reconciled under the Constitution can be so flouted and violated [*sic*].

This rhetoric is only slightly more inflamed than what the tobacco industry has from time to time uttered for public consumption.

There are many brands of cigarettes that advertise low "tar" (ten milligrams or less per cigarette). Why is this a virtue? Because it is the refractory tars in which polycyclic aromatic hydrocarbons and some other carcinogens are concentrated. Aren't the low-tar ads a tacit admission by the tobacco companies that cigarettes indeed cause cancer?

Healthy Buildings International is a for-profit organization, recipient of millions of dollars over the years from the tobacco industry. It performs research on second-hand smoke, and testifies for the tobacco companies. In 1994, three of its technicians complained that senior executives had faked data on inhalable cigarette particles in the air. In every case, the invented or "corrected" data made tobacco smoke seem safer than the technicians' measurements had indicated. Do corporate research departments or outside research contractors ever find a product to be more dangerous than the tobacco corporation has publicly declared? If they do, is their employment continued?

Tobacco is addictive; by many criteria more so than heroin and cocaine. There was a reason people would, as the 1940s ad put it, "walk a mile for a Camel." More people have died of tobacco than in all of World War II. According to the World Health Organization, smoking kills three million people every year worldwide. This will rise to ten million annual deaths by 2020—in part because of a massive advertising campaign to portray smoking as advanced and fashionable to young women in the developing world. Part of the success of the tobacco industry in purveying this brew of addictive poisons can be attributed to widespread unfamiliarity with baloney detection, critical thinking, and the scientific method. Gullibility kills.

---

[1] This is a problem that affects jury trials. Retrospective studies show that some jurors make up their minds very early—perhaps during opening arguments—and then retain the evidence that seems to support their initial impressions and reject the contrary evidence. The method of alternative working hypotheses is not running in their heads.

[2] A more cynical formulation by the Roman historian Polybius:

Since the masses of the people are inconstant, full of unruly desires, passionate, and reckless of consequences, they must be filled with fears to keep them in order. The ancients did well, therefore, to invent gods, and the belief in punishment after death.

[3] My favorite example is this story, told about the Italian physicist Enrico Fermi, newly arrived on American shores, enlisted in the Manhattan nuclear weapons Project, and brought face-to-face in the midst of World War II with U.S. flag officers:

So-and-so is a great general, he was told.
What is the definition of a great general? Fermi characteristically asked.

I guess it's a general who's won many consecutive battles.
How many?
After some back and forth, they settled on five.
What fraction of American generals are great?
After some more back and forth, they settled on a few percent.

But imagine, Fermi rejoined, that there is no such thing as a great general, that all armies are equally matched, and that winning a battle is purely a matter of chance. Then the chance of winning one battle is one out of two, or 1/2; two battles 1/4, three 1/8, four 1/16, and five consecutive battles 1/32—which is about 3 percent. You would *expect* a few percent of American generals to win five consecutive battles—purely by chance. Now, has any of them won *ten* consecutive battles . . . ?

[4]Or: Children who watch violent TV programs tend to be more violent when they grow up. But did the TV cause the violence, or do violent children preferentially enjoy watching violent programs? Very likely both are true. Commercial defenders of TV violence argue that anyone can distinguish between television and reality. But Saturday morning children's programs now average 25 acts of violence per hour. At the very least this desensitizes young children to aggression and random cruelty. And if impressionable adults can have false memories implanted in their brains, what are we implanting in our children when we expose them to some 100,000 acts of violence before they graduate from elementary school?

SPACE IS NUMERIC
1995

Ellen Ullman was involved with high-level computer technology long before it became a national craze and has worked as a software engineer and consultant in California for over twenty years. An expert in her field, she is equally sensitive to the benefits and the drawbacks of the technological revolution. Her personal essays, collected in 1997 in *Close to the Machine: Technophilia and Its Discontents,* explore that tension. Three sections of *Close to the Machine* were presented, in an abbreviated form, on the National Public Radio program "All Things Considered." One reviewer of her book commented, "[Ullman] explores one of the biggest questions of our time: what is it about the numerical, seemingly inhuman world of computing that holds such powerful, wholly human allure?"

I HAVE NO IDEA WHAT TIME IT IS. There are no windows in this office and no clock, only the blinking red LED display of a microwave, which flashes 12:00, 12:00, 12:00, 12:00. Joel and I have been programming for days. We have a bug, a stubborn demon of a bug. So the red pulse no-time feels right, like a read-out of our brains, which have somehow synchronized themselves at the same blink rate.

"But what if they select all the text and—"

"—hit Delete."

"Damn! The NULL case!"

"And if not we're out of the text field and they hit space—"

"—yeah, like for—"

"—no parameter—"

"Hell!"

"So what if we space-pad?"

"I don't know. . . . Wait a minute!"

"Yeah, we could space-pad—"

"—and do space as numeric."

"Yes! We'll call SendKey(space) to—?"

"—the numeric object."

"My God! That fixes it!"

"Yeah! That'll work if—"

"—space is numeric!"

"—if space is numeric!"

We lock eyes. We barely breathe. For a slim moment, we are together in a universe where two human beings can simultaneously understand the statement "if space is numeric!"

Joel and I started this round of debugging on Friday morning. Sometime later, maybe Friday night, another programmer, Danny, came to work. I suppose it must be Sunday by now because it's been a while since we've seen my client's employees around the office. Along the way, at odd times of day or night that have completely escaped us, we've ordered in three meals of Chinese food, eaten six large pizzas, consumed several beers, had innumerable bottles of fizzy water, and finished two entire bottles of wine. It has occurred to me that if people really knew how software got written, I'm not sure if they'd give their money to a bank or get on an airplane ever again.

What are we working on? An artificial intelligence project to find "subversive" talk over international phone lines? Software for the second start-up of a Silicon Valley executive banished from his first company? A system to help AIDS patients get services across a city? The details escape me just now. We may be helping poor sick people or tuning a set of low-level routines to verify bits on a distributed database protocol—I don't care. I should care; in another part of my being—later, perhaps when we emerge from this room full of computers—I will care very much why and for whom and for what purpose I am writing software. But just now: no. I have passed through a membrane where the real world and its uses no longer matter. I am a software engineer, an independent contractor working for a department of a city government. I've hired Joel and three other programmers to work with me. Down the hall is Danny, a slim guy in wire-rimmed glasses who comes to work with a big, wire-haired dog. Across the bay in his converted backyard shed is Mark, who works on the database. Somewhere, probably asleep by now, is Bill the network guy. Right now, there are only two things in the universe that matter to us. One, we have some bad bugs to fix. Two, we're supposed to install the system on Monday, which I think is tomorrow.

"Oh, no, no!" moans Joel, who is slumped over his keyboard. "No-*o-o-o*." It comes out in a long wail. It has the sound of lost love, lifetime regret. We've both been programmers long enough to know that we are at *that place*. If we find one more serious problem we can't solve right away, we will not make it. We won't install. We'll go the terrible, familiar way of all software: we'll be late.

"No, no, no, no. What if the members of the set start with spaces. Oh, God. It won't work."

He is as near to naked despair as has ever been shown to me by anyone not in a film. Here, in *that place,* we have no shame. He has seen me sleeping on the floor, drooling. We have both seen Danny's puffy white midsection—young as he is, it's a pity—when he stripped to his underwear in the heat of the machine room. I have seen Joel's dandruff, light coating of cat fur on his clothes, noticed things about his body I should not. And I'm sure he's seen my sticky hair, noticed how dull I look without make-up, caught sight of other details too intimate to mention. Still, none of this matters anymore. Our bodies were abandoned long ago, reduced to hunger and sleeplessness and the ravages of sitting for hours at a keyboard and a mouse. Our physical selves have been battered away. Now we know each other in one way and one way only: the code.

Besides, I know I can now give him pleasure of an order which is rare in any life: I am about to save him from despair.

"No problem," I say evenly. I put my hand on his shoulder, intending a gesture of reassurance. "The parameters *never* start with a space."

It is just as I hoped. His despair vanishes. He becomes electric, turns to the keyboard and begins to type at a rapid speed. Now he is gone from me. He is disappearing into the code— now that he knows it will work, now that I have reassured him that, in our universe, the one we created together, space can indeed be forever and reliably numeric.

The connection, the shared thought-stream, is cut. It has all the frustration of being abandoned by a lover just before climax. I know this is not physical love. He is too young, he works for me; he's a man and I've been tending toward women; in any case, he's too prim and business-schooled for my tastes. I know this sensation is not *real* attraction: it is only the spillover, the excess charge, of the mind back into the abandoned body. *Only.* Ha. This is another real-world thing that does not matter. My entire self wants to melt into this brilliant, electric being who has shared his mind with me for twenty seconds.

Restless, I go into the next room where Danny is slouched at his keyboard. The big, wire-haired dog growls at me. Danny looks up, scowls like his dog, then goes back to typing. I am the designer of this system, his boss on this project. But he's not even trying to hide his contempt. Normal programmer, I think. He has fifteen windows full of code open on his desktop. He has overpopulated his eyes, thoughts, imagination. He is drowning in bugs and I know I could help him, but he wants me dead just at the moment. I am the last-straw irritant. *Talking:* Shit! What the hell is wrong with me? Why would I want to *talk* to him? Can't I see that his stack is overflowing?

"Joel may have the overlapping controls working," I say.

"Oh, yeah?" He doesn't look up.

"He's been using me as a programming dummy," I say. "Do you want to talk me through the navigation errors?" Navigation errors: bad. You click to go somewhere but get somewhere else. Very, very bad.

"What?" He pretends not to hear me.

"Navigation errors. How are they?"

"I'm working on them." Huge, hateful scowl. Contempt that one human being should not express to another under any circumstances. Hostility that should kill me, if I were not used to it, familiar with it, practiced in receiving it. Besides, we are at *that place.* I know that this hateful programmer is all I have between me and the navigation bug. "I'll come back later," I say.

Later: how much later can it get? Daylight can't be far off now. This small shoal of pre-installation madness is washing away even as I wander back down the hall to Joel.

"Yes! It's working!" says Joel, hearing my approach.

He looks up at me. "You were right," he says. The ultimate one programmer can say to another, the accolade given so rarely as to be almost unknown in our species. He looks right at me as he says it: "You were right. As always."

This is beyond rare. *Right:* the thing a programmer desires above, beyond all. *As always:* unspeakable incalculable gift.

"I could not have been right without you," I say. This is true beyond question. "I only opened the door. You figured out how to go through."

I immediately see a certain perfume advertisement: a man holding a violin embraces a woman at a piano. I want to be that ad. I want efficacies of reality to vanish, and I want to be the man with violin, my programmer to be the woman at the piano. As in the ad, I want the teacher to interrupt the lesson and embrace the student. I want the rules to be broken. Tabu. That is the name of the perfume. I want to do what is taboo. I am the boss, the senior, the employer, the person in charge. So I must not touch him. It is all taboo. Still—

Danny appears in the doorway.

"The navigation bug is fixed. I'm going home."

"I'll test it—"

"It's fixed."

He leaves.

It is sometime in the early morning. Joel and I are not sure if the night guard is still on duty. If we leave, we may not get back up the elevator. We leave anyway.

We find ourselves on the street in a light drizzle. He has on a raincoat, one that he usually wears over his too-prim, too-straight, good-biz-school suits. I have on a second-hand-store leather bomber jacket, black beret, boots. Someone walking by might wonder what we were doing together at this still-dark hour of the morning.

"Goodnight," I say. We're still charged with thought energy. I don't dare extend my hand to shake his.

"Goodnight," he says.

We stand awkwardly for two beats more. "This will sound strange," he says, "but I hope I don't see you tomorrow."

We stare at each other, still drifting in the wake of our shared mind-stream. I know exactly what he means. We will only see each other tomorrow if I find a really bad bug.

"Not strange at all," I say, "I hope I don't see you, either."

I don't see him. The next day, I find a few minor bugs, fix them, and decide the software is good enough. Mind-meld fantasies recede as the system goes live. We install the beginnings of a city-wide registration system for AIDS patients. Instead of carrying around soiled and wrinkled eligibility documents, AIDS clients only have to prove once that they are really sick and really poor. It is an odd system, if I think of it, certifying that people are truly desperate in the face of possible death.

Still, this time I'm working on a "good" project, I tell myself. We are *helping* people, say the programmers over and over, nearly in disbelief at their good fortune. Three programmers, the network guy, me—fifty-eight years of collective technical experience—and the idea of helping people with a computer is a first for any of us.

Yet I am continually anxious. How do we protect this database full of the names of people with AIDS? Is a million-dollar computer system the best use of continually shrinking funds? It was easier when I didn't have to think about the real-world effect of my work. It was easier—and I got paid more—when I was writing an "abstracted interface to any arbitrary input device." When I was designing a "user interface paradigm," defining a "test-bed methodology." I could disappear into weird passions of logic. I could stay in a world peopled entirely by programmers, other weird logic-dreamers like myself, all caught up in our own inner electricities. It was easier and more valued. In my profession, software engineering, there is something almost shameful in this helpful, social services system we're building. The whole project smacks of "end users"—those contemptible, oblivious people who just want to use the stuff we write and don't care how we did it.

"What are you working on?" asked an acquaintance I ran into at a book signing. She's a woman with her own start-up company. Her offices used to be in the loft just below mine, two blocks from South Park, in San Francisco's Multimedia Gulch. She is tall and strikingly attractive; she wears hip, fashionable clothes; her company already has its first million in venture-capital funding. "What are you working on," she wanted to know, "I mean, that isn't under non-D?"

Under non-D. Nondisclosure. That's the cool thing to be doing: working on a system so new, so just started-up, that you can't talk about it under pain of lawsuit.

"Oh, not much," I answered, trying to sound breezy. A city-wide network for AIDS service providers: how unhip could I get? If I wanted to do something for people with AIDS, I should make my first ten million in stock options, then attend some fancy party where I wear a red ribbon on my chest. I should be a sponsor for Digital Queers. But actually working on a project for end users? Where my client is a government agency? In the libertarian world of computing, where "creating wealth" is all, I am worse than uncool: I am aiding and abetting the bureaucracy, I am a net consumer of federal taxes—I'm what's wrong with this country.

"Oh, I'm basically just plugging in other people's software these days. Not much engineering. You know," I waved vaguely, "*plumbing* mostly."

My vagueness paid off. The woman winked at me. "Networks," she said.

"Yeah. Something like that," I said. I was disgusted with myself, but, when she walked away, I was relieved.

The end users I was so ashamed of came late in the system development process. I didn't meet them until the software was half-written. This is not how these things are supposed to go—the system is not supposed to predate the people who will use it—but it often goes that way anyhow.

The project was eight months old when my client-contact, a project manager in a city department, a business-like woman of fifty, finally set up a meeting. Representatives of several social-service agencies were invited; eight came. A printed agenda was handed around the conference table. The first item was "Review agenda." My programmer-mind whirred at the implication of endless reiteration: Agenda. Review agenda. Agenda. Forever.

"Who dreamed up this stuff?" asked a woman who directed a hospice and home-care agency. "This is all useless!" We had finally come to item four on the agenda: "Review System Specifications." The hospice director waved a big stack of paper—the specifications arrived at by a "task force"—then tossed it across the table. A heavy-set woman apparently of Middle Eastern descent, she had probably smoked a very large number of cigarettes in the course of her fifty-odd years on earth. Her laugh trailed off into a chesty rumble, which she used as a kind of drum roll to finish off her scorn.

The other users were no more impressed. A black woman who ran a shelter—elegant, trailing Kente cloth. She arranged her acres of fabric as some sort of displacement for her boredom; each time I started talking, I seemed to have to speak over a high jangle of her many bracelets set to play as she, ignoring me with something that was not quite hostility, arranged and rearranged herself. A woman who ran a clinic for lesbians, a self-described "femme" with hennaed hair and red fingernails: "Why didn't someone come talk to us first?" she asked. A good question. My client sat shamefaced. A young, handsome black man, assistant to the hospice director, quick and smart: he simply shook his head and kept a skeptical smile on his face. Finally a dentist and a doctor, two white males who looked pale and watery in this sea of diversity: they worried that the system would get in the way of giving services. And around the table they went, complaint by complaint.

I started to panic. Before this meeting, the users existed only in my mind, projections, all mine. They were abstractions, the initiators of tasks that set off remote procedure calls; triggers to a set of logical and machine events that ended in an update to a relational database on a central server. Now I was confronted with their fleshly existence. And now I had to think about the actual existence of the people who used the services delivered by the users' agencies, sick people who were no fools, who would do what they needed to do to get pills, food vouchers, a place to sleep.

I wished, earnestly, I could just replace the abstractions with the actual people. But it was already too late for that. The system pre-existed the people. Screens were prototyped. Data elements were defined. The machine events already had more reality, had been with me longer, than the human beings at the conference table. Immediately, I saw it was a problem not of replacing one reality with another but of two realities. I was there at the edge: the interface of the system, in all its existence, to the people, in all their existence.

I talked, asked questions, but I saw I was operating at a different speed from the people at the table. Notch down, I told myself. *Notch down.* The users were bright, all too sensitive to each other's feelings. Anyone who was the slightest bit cut off was gotten back to sweetly: "You were saying?" Their courtesy was structural, built into their "process." I had to keep my hand over my mouth to keep from jumping in. Notch down, I told myself again. *Slow down.* But it was not working. My brain whirred out a stream of logic-speak: "The agency sees the client records if and only if there is a relationship defined between the agency and the client," I heard myself saying. "By definition, as soon as the client receives services from the agency, the system considers the client to have a relationship with the provider. An internal index is created which represents the relationship." The hospice director closed her eyes to concentrate. She would have smoked if she could have; she looked at me as if through something she had just exhaled.

I took notes, pages of revisions that had to be done immediately or else doom the system to instant disuse. The system had no life without the user, I saw. I'd like to say that I was instantly converted to the notion of real human need, to the impact I would have on the working lives of these people at the table, on the people living with AIDS; I'd like to claim a sudden sense of real-world responsibility. But that would be lying. What I really thought was this: I must save the system.

I ran off to call the programmers. Living in my hugely different world from the sick patients, the forbearing service providers, the earnest and caring users at the meeting, I didn't wait to find a regular phone. I went into the next room, took out my cell phone, began punching numbers into it, and hit the "send" button: "We have to talk," I said.

By the time I saw Joel, Danny, and Mark, I had reduced the users' objections to a set of five system changes. I would like to use the word "reduce" like a cook: something boiled down to its essence. But I was aware that the real human essence was already absent from the list I'd prepared. An item like "How will we know if the clients have TB?"—the fear of sitting in a small, poorly ventilated room with someone who has medication-resistant TB, the normal and complicated biological urgency of that question— became a list of data elements to be added to the screens and the database. I tried to communicate some of the sense of the meeting to the programmers. They were interested, but in a mild, backgrounded way. Immediately, they seized the list of changes and, as I watched, they turned them into further abstractions,

"We can add a parameter to the remote procedure call."

"We should check the referential integrity on that."

"Should the code be attached to that control or should it be in global scope?"

"Global, because this other object here needs to know about the condition."

"No! No globals. We agreed. No more globals!"

We have entered the code zone. Here thought is telegraphic and exquisitely precise. I feel no need to slow myself down. On the contrary, the faster the better. Joel runs off a stream of detail, and halfway through a sentence, Mark, the database programmer, completes the thought. I mention a screen element, and Danny, who programs the desktop software, thinks of two elements I've forgotten. Mark will later say all bugs are Danny's fault, but, for now, they work together like cheerful little parallel-processing machines, breaking the problem into pieces that they attack simultaneously. Danny will later become the angry programmer scowling at me from behind his broken code, but now he is still a jovial guy with wire-rimmed glasses and a dog that accompanies him everywhere. "Neato," he says to something Mark has proposed, grinning, patting the dog, happy as a clam.

"Should we modify the call to AddUser—"

"—to check for UserType—"

"Or should we add a new procedure call—"

"—something like ModifyPermissions."

"But won't that add a new set of data elements that repeat—"

"Yeah, a repeating set—"

"—which we'll have to—"

"—renormalize!"

Procedure calls. Relational database normalization. Objects going in and out of scope. Though my mind is racing, I feel calm. It's the spacey calm of satellites speeding over the earth at a thousand miles per second: relative to each other, we float. The images of patients with AIDS recede, the beleaguered service providers are forgotten, the whole grim reality of the epidemic fades. We give ourselves over to the sheer fun of the technical, to the nearly sexual pleasure of the clicking thought-stream.

Some part of me mourns, but I know there is no other way: human needs must cross the line into code. They must pass through this semipermeable membrane where urgency, fear, and hope are filtered out, and only reason travels across. There is no other way. Real, death-inducing viruses do not travel here. Actual human confusions cannot live here. Everything we want accomplished, everything the system is to provide, must be denatured in its crossing to the machine, or else the system will die.

Opal Palmer Adisa

LYING IN THE TALL GRASSES, EATING CANE
1998

A teacher and the author of several volumes of poetry and short stories, Opal Palmer Adisa won the American Book Award in 1992 for *Tamarind and Mango Women*. Her most recent novel is *It Begins and Ends with Tears* (1997). A resident of California, Adisa writes and lectures frequently on Caribbean culture and her native Jamaica and leads workshops on multiculturalism. "Lying in the Tall Grasses, Eating Cane" takes a place as part of a long tradition of Western prose in which the author reflects on early influences and the process of becoming a writer; in Adisa's case, that odyssey has also involved confronting stereotypes about black women and the assumptions underlying a white male literary history. "Lying in the Tall Grasses, Eating Cane" was first published in the San Francisco literary magazine *ZYZZYVA*.

T HE FIRST STORIES I WROTE were all composed while I lay nestled in the tall grasses, peeling away the sharp skin of the cane with my teeth and feeling deep pleasure as the sweet, sticky juice trickled down my cheeks onto my neck. I would stay concealed by the tall grasses for hours, gazing up at the clouds, observing the shapes of cows, birds, one animal after another dissolving and transforming into another. The heat of the sun penetrated my skin, and the chalky, gauze-like clouds dazzled my eyes, and words as liquid as cane juice, as comforting as the tall grasses, came to me.

When I turned eight years old, I started to compose stories and poems on paper, but I never shared them with anyone. I was just beginning my dance with words; they were as sweet and sensual as the chocolate bars I held in my mouth until they melted, gluing my tongue to the roof of my mouth and leaving my fingers stained a sticky brown. Writing was just for me; it was my secret, like my favorite places to go off to be alone. I often wandered aimlessly over my community with its immense space dotted with large cotton trees, tenanted by acres and acres of cane and banana fields, many connecting canals and dense forest where numerous species of lizards, birds, and other critters dwelled. I recorded almost all I saw and stored the rest in my memory. I felt an urgency and deep need to do this. Mostly, I felt the people around me did not perceive their own immense beauty and truth.

Almost every Sunday my family went to the beach. There I would pass hours splashing in the water, lying by the shore allowing the ebb and flow of the waves to wash over me, building sand castles, rubbing sand all over my body, and listening intently to the chatter of the ocean. The first poem I had published, at thirteen, was entitled "The Sounds I Like to Hear." The roar and caw of the sea was the dominant image. However, the abundant glee of the wind rustling through trees, flapping clothes on lines, swirling dust into the air, and awakening my skin, also resonated throughout the poem. I was attracted to sounds—mosquitoes buzzing, lizards croaking, and dogs yapping in rounds at night. Colors mesmerized me—verdant mountain ranges perched against aqua skies, purple-hued skin touched off by an indigo shirt, a cinnamon-toned face regaled in a golden hat.

Movements caught hold of my breath—the gait of youths on their way to a soccer match, market women balancing huge baskets on their heads, cane cutters dancing with the swing of their machetes. I was also enthralled by the deep, full laughter of people and the way they fervently clung to their beliefs. I always nestled in some corner, being seen and not heard, taking in the talk of the "big" people. I was greedy for their stories; my hunger was never satiated. The relationships between people fascinated me, but I was more intrigued by what was not said, gestures that belied words. I was drawn to the working class and their open display of emotions. The women were particularly dramatic. When angered or hurt, they would shout to attract an audience, their arms akimbo, their very stance daring the person who wronged them to step over the boundary they had defined. They often solicited fights to appease their wounded feelings. I always stood on the fringes, entranced, trying to make sense of such wanton displays of emotions. My middle-class mother was preaching just the opposite: restraint, quiet, lady-like behavior. Whereas the middle class appeared to suck in their pain until they became bitter, the working class was unabashed. I would often sneak off so I could be with them, to listen in on their conversation, to drink in their zest for life, to observe their every action. They lived life with a robust intensity that tingled me to the core. I searched my mind for words, language with which to convey the intensity of their feelings, but believed myself to be sadly lacking. So I stored their stories in the recesses of my mind.

But that did not make me a writer. I never thought of myself as a writer, I suppose as a result of being reared in a colonial society with a British education that vociferously denounced Jamaica's cultural ethos. In fact, we were presumed to lack history and therefore had nothing worthwhile to write about. I always suspected this history I was being taught was somehow erroneous or at best lopsided and suspect. I didn't feel wrong or inferior, yet my education was telling me that even the way we Jamaicans spoke was wrong. I remember my teachers drilling me to speak the Queen's English. All the books I read and the poems I memorized were by British or American poets, almost all of whom were men, and presumably dead. At that time, I truly believed that a writer was synonymous with death.

One had to die to be a writer, and I was not prepared to die, even for the glory of seeing my words in print. More important, I believed only people who lived elsewhere, and who talked about sleet, which I could not imagine, and watched daffodils, were writers. I had not yet read Claude McKay's "The Tropics in New York" in which bananas, tangerines and mangoes, emblems of my culture, are mentioned, even elevated. Although my family boasted a large library, and my mother and sister were avid readers, I can say with perfect honesty that I never read a book or poem by a black person, from anywhere in the world, until I was sixteen and had moved to New York. There, while completing a year of high school, I was introduced to Langston Hughes, Gwendolyn Brooks, and Jean Toomer.

Toomer's *Cane* is the single text that is most responsible for me recognizing and answering the call of a writer. The title attracted me, and I was captured completely by Toomer's lyrical surrealism that transported me to a familiar terrain, reminiscent of the sugar estate on which my navel-string was buried. Like the Jamaica of my childhood, Toomer's *Cane* was inhabited by black people with their everyday extraordinary simplicity and grace. I knew in that moment, upon completing that volume, that I wanted to write, not in the surreptitious manner that I had been engaged in all along, but openly, to share with others.

Those African American writers led me to discover Caribbean and African writers when I entered Hunter College. I was amazed and also angry that it took me so long to discover these writers, many of whom were Jamaicans, and most of whom had been writing before I was born. Why did it take me eighteen years to discover them, and then so far from home? From then on, I read avidly, and tentatively began to seek out black writers in New York.

In my nineteenth year, two events set me firmly on my course to being a writer. First, I met LeRoy Clarke, a Trinidadian painter and poet. When I told him I wrote, he invited me to show him my work. He was surprised when the following week I handed him three folders with almost two hundred poems. Nonetheless, he took and read them. Then he called me up and declared that I was a poet. Clarke recommended that I rework some of the poems and suggested that I attend readings regularly. Second, I had the good fortune to hear Sonia Sanchez read. There before me was a black woman, as petite as me, spewing fiery words, resonating truth. Meeting Clarke and seeing Sanchez read launched my career. The fear I always harbored about sharing my work receded, and I found my voice reading at open mikes. I was amazed when people came up to me afterward and said they liked my poems and urged me to submit my work for publication.

By the time I returned to Jamaica six years later, armed with a B.A. degree, things had changed. Books by Caribbean writers were being taught in the schools, and the poetry scene was vibrant. I was fortunate to be mentored by Mervyn Morris and Kamau Brathwaite, who were teaching at the University of the West Indies, and whose love and guidance I still value. I wrote and hosted a poetry program on one of the radio stations that featured the works of published as well as unpublished writers. My poems were published almost weekly for three years in the Sunday literary section of one of the newspapers. I wrote feverishly. I continued to observe my people, and, with the shift in education, there was a shift in the importance of the Jamaican language. I began to experiment and incorporate my mother tongue into my work. I remembered the dialect poetry of Louise Bennett, which I had heard all throughout my childhood, and wondered why I had not before considered her poetry on equal footing with Longfellow's, for instance. Studying Bennett's work for the first time strengthened my resolve to incorporate the Jamaican language into my work, *me could labrish and write fi we yarns.*

I have been writing now for over twenty years. I call myself
a writer, but sometimes I question whether or not I am a full-
fledged writer. I have written more poems than I can count or
that will ever be published, and I have four books to my credit.
But I have never given writing first priority. It is still what I do
after I have done everything else, the last thing I get to after I
have taken care of my children, cleaned my house, marked my
students' papers, and answered numerous telephone calls. I have
not given this long-standing, faithful lover, this passionate devo-
tee, my full attention. In some respect, I still fear what might
happen to the rest of my life if I were to abandon myself to this
paramour. In many ways, I sense that the depth of my feelings
borders on sickness; yet I am also painfully aware that this lover
is as necessary as the blood that feeds my heart.

The memory of the grass tickling my skin, the sun pressing
the clothes to my body, the sweetness of the cane juice in my
mouth, and the clear blue skies peering down at me are still very
vivid. These images, along with the vibrant energy of my people, continue to fuel my work, and I pray they will never abandon me. I cannot not write. I am still an apprentice, kneeling at
the foot of this god.

> i didn't choose this lover
> it was not i who went
> in search of his ardor
> believe me
> i ignored him
> for as long as i could
> but he always shadowed me
>
> then one day
> when all the glow
> was sucked from the sun
> when tears were a brine

on my cheeks
he came to me
not open
like a friend
offering comfort
not stealthily
like a desperate thief
but like an animal
tracking my smell

i was vulnerable
you must understand
i needed to hear
someone say
i was special
i needed to feel
as if i was important
worthy of someone's love

so i opened my arms
and he pressed his body
to my chest
blew sultry breath on my neck
caressed the muscles in my lower back
and his kisses
how to describe the confectionery
sweetness of his tongue
in my mouth
the soothing warmth
of his hands
caressing   luring
opening me up

i didn't want

this lover
truly
my affection had been unrequited
for many years
for i suspected
always knew
should i slip
should i allow this lover
to get hold of my hand
to gaze into my face
that i would never be able
to free myself from him
that he would forever
be in my bed
every word i speak
from there on
would only mouth his desires

it's dangerous
but wonderful
my work   this lover

i'm lost
christened writer
truly i am
to this suitor

i am a writer